Alaska to Nunavut

THE GREAT RIVERS

Neil Hartling *with Photographs by Terry Parker*

KEY PORTER BOOKS

National Library of Canada Cataloguing in Publication

Hartling, Neil

Alaska to Nunavut : the great rivers / text by Neil Hartling ; photography by Terry Parker.

Includes bibliographical references.

ISBN 1-55263-515-5

1. Rivers—Canada, Northern. 2. Rivers—Alaska. 3. Natural history—Canada, Northern. 4. Natural history—Alaska. 5. Canada, Northern—Description and travel. 6. Alaska—Description and travel.

I. Parker, Terry II. Title.

E41.H373 2003   917.904'3   C2003-902100-9

The publisher gratefully acknowledges the support of the Canada Council for the Arts and the Ontario Arts Council for its publishing program.

We acknowledge the financial support of the Government of Canada through the Book Publishing Industry Development Program (BPIDP) for our publishing activities.

Key Porter Books Limited
Six Adelaide Street East,
Toronto, Ontario
Canada M5C 1H6

www.keyporter.com

Design: Peter Maher
Electronic formatting: Jean Peters
Maps: John Lightfoot

Printed and bound in Hong Kong

05 06 07 5 4 3 2

Please Note…
This book is a photo-narrative, not a guidebook. The author, photographer, publisher, and associated contributors assume no responsibility for injury or loss that may result from practical implementation of the information found within.

CAPTION FOR PAGE II: *A long time-exposure calms the fast moving water of Bloody Falls-Coppermine River, Nunavut.*

CPAWS-Yukon is a conservation organization dedicated to promoting awareness, understanding and enjoyment of the inherent values of northern wildlands through education and experience.

Contents

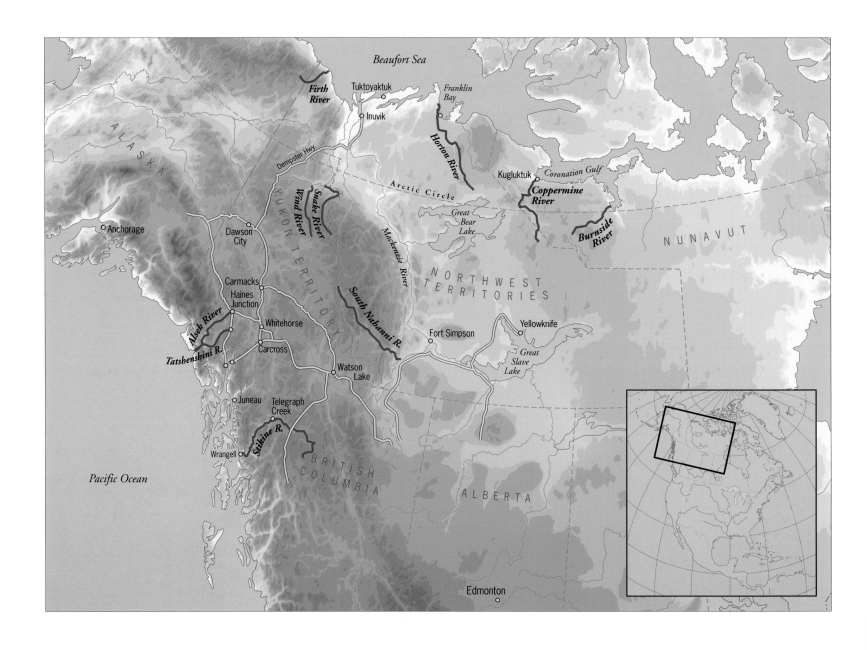

Beaufort Sea

Firth River

Tuktoyaktuk

Franklin Bay

Inuvik

Horton River

Coronation Gulf

Kugluktuk

Coppermine River

ALASKA

Dempster Hwy.

Arctic Circle

Great Bear Lake

Burnside River

NUNAVUT

Anchorage

Snake River

Wind River

Dawson City

YUKON TERRITORY

Mackenzie River

N O R T H W E S T

T E R R I T O R I E S

Carmacks

Haines Junction

South Nahanni R.

Fort Simpson

Yellowknife

Alsek River

Whitehorse

Carcross

Tatshenshini R.

Watson Lake

Great Slave Lake

Juneau

Telegraph Creek

Stikine R.

Wrangell

BRITISH COLUMBIA

ALBERTA

Pacific Ocean

Edmonton

Of all the changes that will come to Canada in the next generation, we must prevent any of a sort that will diminish the essential beauty of this country. For if that beauty is lost, or if that wilderness escapes, the very nature and character of this land will have passed beyond our grasp.

—Pierre Elliott Trudeau
Former prime minister of Canada,
aficionado of wild rivers.

Introduction: The Headwaters

Canada has been described as a country designed to be traveled by canoe. The sinuous waterways that lace the land together form arteries of life and movement. Coursing from the heart of the land, delivering nourishment to the extremities, our rivers are conduits of sustenance. Flowing beneath glacier-crested mountain peaks, through boreal forest, taiga, across tundra, saturated in color with wildflowers and teeming with wildlife, they are also a feast for the eyes and a balm for the heart and soul. From Alaska to Nunavut, I have had the privilege of outfitting and guiding journeys by canoe and raft on our northern waterways for two decades. It has been my good fortune that Terry Parker has accompanied many of these sojourns to photograph the stunning sights found there.

Terry's artistry demonstrates that these rivers are settings of drama and beauty. In addition, his images underscore the realities of the northern landscape through which the rivers flow: great distances, ecological sensitivity, sparse population, indigenous people, political boundaries, and diversity of regions. His photographs reflect his sensitivity to, and love for, these rivers and the wild lands through which they flow. Most

profoundly, through his images, he can get you "inside the skin" of their creatures.

It is a challenging task to distil these waterways into words, although, I have often said that one of the few things I enjoy as much as paddling a wilderness river is talking and writing about it. Thankfully, "a picture is worth a thousand words," as the old adage says. This book is a labor of love. The stories are told by a river guide who is hopelessly enchanted with this land.

Although we consider these rivers to flow through uninhabited wilderness, humans have dwelt in these regions for thousands of years, creating a rich history. These indigenous cultures are referred to collectively in Canada as "First Nations." While I have tried to shed light on their past, you will have to visit the North to experience the rich tapestry of First Nations stories. These tales are carefully and accurately passed down through generations via oral tradition. They belong to the teller and have layers of meaning. The ownership of the story could be compared to our version of copyright. The stories hold deep significance to the culture and transcend physical and spiritual meaning. In a culture that has always practiced holistic medicine, they say, "story telling is the ointment of the healer." It would

The Tatshenshini swells in size and speed as it courses through the St. Elias Range.

~~~~~~~~~~~~~~~~~~~~~~~~~~~~~~~~~
~~~~~~~~~~~~~~~~~~~~~~~~~~~~~~~~~

be presumptuous of me to recount such tales here, but happily, Terry's images portray the elements, drama, and inspiration behind the stories.

Unfortunately this is not an exhaustive survey of the great northern rivers of North America. The Back, Hanbury, Thelon, Bonnet Plume, Hood, Mountain, Kongakut, Seal, Soper, Kazan, Slave, Taku and others all have significant features but must await another volume. Fortunately the rivers that Terry has had the opportunity to explore are considered the "crème de la crème" of northern waterways. The images have been collected over more than a decade on the river trips that we share with our southern guests. While the northern landscape can seem austere, it is accessible and the rivers serve as the perfect way to travel through the land and experience its many wonders—to say nothing of enjoying the vacation of a lifetime!

All this said, it is critical that we not lose sight of the life-giving qualities of all waterways. The boreal forest and tundra are laced with them. The lowly creek, bereft of canyons or waterfalls, shrouded in willows, remains a vital artery of the surrounding land and life.

Perhaps one of the greatest testimonies to the appeal of our northern rivers comes from my past clients, who return year after year to visit yet another river destination. I have witnessed the ultimate tribute to these waterways over the years when former clients have passed away and recorded in their wills that their ashes be spread at a cherished place on one of these rivers.

These northern rivers have been good to me and have brought health and happiness to my life. I hope that they may do the same for you.

NEIL HARTLING
Whitehorse, Yukon
2003

Alpine Forget-me-nots.

5

CHAPTER 1

South Nahanni River (Northwest Territories): River of Gold

Those of us who had the good fortune to be on the South Nahanni in those last days of the old North may, in times of hunger or hardship, have cursed the day we ever heard the name of that fabled river. Yet a treasure was ours in the end: memories of a carefree time and utter and absolute freedom which the years cannot dim nor the present age provide.
—RAYMOND PATTERSON IN *DANGEROUS RIVER*

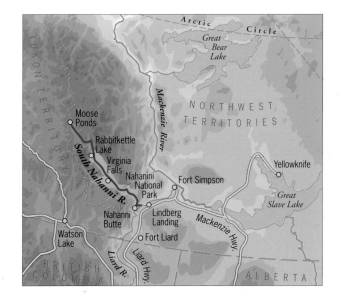

It is difficult to describe one of the most famous rivers in the world without a string of superlatives, for indeed, the Nahanni lives up to its larger-than-life reputation.

As the first Canadian World Heritage Site of UNESCO and the most spectacular waterway of the Canadian Heritage Rivers System, the Nahanni is an icon of wild Canadian rivers and our wilderness. To this day the South Nahanni watershed remains an isolated

The view atop Sunblood Mountain. A rigorous day hike from Virginia Falls brings you to a panoramic view—upriver and down. The meandering nature of the river above the falls reveals the fact that Nahanni is an ancient river that pre-dates the surrounding mountains. It is referred to as an antecedent river; a prairie river in a mountainous landscape.

region. Most of the area's mountains are nameless; those that have names allude to the region's mysterious past: Deadmen Valley, Headless Creek, Funeral Range, Sombre Mountains, Hells Gate— all speak of a land of myth and romance. Sharp granite peaks stand guard to the west. It is a place where clouds drifting below the mountain tops and canyon rim redefine the relationship with earth, sky, and water.

What of the legend, myth, and romance? Much of this stems from the turn of the last century in the Gold Rush era. R.M. Patterson, author of *Dangerous River*,

OPPOSITE PAGE: *Nimble-footed Dall's sheep on a canyon ledge. These sheep count on a "vertical world" for security, and are masters of the slopes.*

LEFT: *Virginia Falls— nearly twice the height of Niagara Falls.* Nailicho *is their Dene name. The center spire of harder rock that splits the flow is referred to by canoeists as Mason's Rock. Bill Mason was a filmmaker, artist, and an environmentalist who did much to educate the public about wild rivers and wild places. The falls were named after the daughter of American explorer Fenlay Hunter in 1928.*

Origin: the Moose Ponds on the border of the Northwest Territories and the Yukon Territory
Length: 310 miles (500 km)
Drop: 3,000 feet (915 m)
Completion: Confluence with the Liard River
Unique Status: Creation of Nahanni National Park, 1972. One of the first UNESCO World Heritage Sites—1978, Canadian Heritage River, 1984.

Gravel bars of yellow dryas.

In 1947, the Nahanni was embedded in the psyche of the nation by a young journalist, who would later become famous. Pierre Berton's syndicated stories launched his career as a writer and etched the lore of the Nahanni indelibly on the consciousness of Canadians. Decades later, in 1970, Prime Minister Pierre Elliott Trudeau traveled the river. His visit became instrumental in the subsequent designation of the area as Nahanni National Park Reserve in 1972. This designation put an end to proposed hydroelectric developments that would have silenced Virginia Falls and flooded the magnificent canyons downstream. Royalty such as Prince Andrew, a governor general, premiers, and a stream of other luminaries, have subsequently visited the Nahanni, heightening the profile and reputation of the stately river.

Beginning at the tiny Moose Ponds, perched high on the continental divide, the river plunges through a backdrop of alpine scenery, winding its way through a maze of boulder-choked rapids which are challenging to navigate. This portion is appropriately known as "The Rock Gardens." One hundred and six miles (170 km) later the channel swells in size and becomes more navigable. It is here that Hot Springs Valley and Rabbitkettle Lake mark the beginning of Nahanni National Park.

Secrets of the millennia unfold at Rabbitkettle Lake and Hot Springs Valley. Geological clues reveal the unique tale of a land that was mostly spared from the scouring of the last Ice Age. Not far from the lake,

referred to this time as "a period of romantic buffoonery." Ill-fated prospecting expeditions led to colorful place names, and for a time the entire area was referred to as Headless Valley.

Rabbitkettle Hotsprings has created Canada's largest tufa mounds—high terraces of soft calcium, which are nearly half the size of a football field. From faults in the earth's crust, hot sulfurous water laden with dissolved calcium gurgle to the surface. As the streams trickle off the mounds, they leave behind fragile carbonate terraces. These are so delicate that even footsteps can erode

Camping in the depths of the canyons is a humbling experience. The walls, soaring overhead, close out the sky and seem capable of folding you into the earth. The strata of walls parade eons of earth history in the deepest canyons "north of sixty" anywhere in the world.

them; and hikers must tread lightly on these natural wonders, barefooted and in the accompaniment of a park interpreter.

To the west are the sharp granite spires of the Ragged Range. Two hundred million years ago, the molten granite was pushed upwards from a flat plain, creating the jagged mountains of hard rock. Currently this region of dramatic spires and world-class climbing lies outside the park boundary. It is hoped that in a proposed park expansion, this region will be included in Nahanni. The up-thrusting of these mountains caused the folding of the surrounding, softer sedimentary rock of the ancient seabeds. These ranges are the Mackenzie Mountains through which the Nahanni flows.

Nahanni camp kitchen. The use of environmental fire boxes is mandatory. While prevention of fire scars is the prime objective, guides prefer them as they require less wood and the sheltered, focused flame cooks food efficiently. The steady supply of driftwood provides an environmentally friendly fuel source.

As it winds below Rabbitkettle Lake, Nahanni's swift but flat current does not betray the fury ahead at Virginia Falls. Perched on a mossy outcrop overlooking the falls, it is easy to loose yourself in the vast and explosive display of water in motion. The Sluice Box Rapids run for half a mile (1 km) leading to the brink

Unlike younger mountain rivers, the Nahanni does not cut a narrow straight course. Before the formation of the mountains, the Nahanni was a river of the flat plain, meandering in broad sweeps as a prairie river does. As the Mackenzie Mountains rose, the river cut across the grain of the land. The earth actually rose while the river held its own against the change. This process took place over roughly 1.4 million years. The result is a meandering prairie river in a mountain landscape. The Nahanni is termed an antecedent river because it preceded the surrounding mountains. Unlike many Canadian rivers, it's been flowing since long before the Ice Ages.

In spite of meandering, the Nahanni is attempting to straighten the canyons and, to some extent, is succeeding. The heights of the canyon display the evolution graphically. Overhead, cutting in and out of the canyon wall, one can see the remains of two abandoned meanders. These former twisting channels were left high above the river as the land rose around the river.

Running the rapids of Painted Canyon below Virginia Falls. This gorge was created by the eroding action of the falls.

of the drop. Plumes of water erupt skywards as the river plummets over a drop nearly twice the height of Niagara Falls. Over time, this cataract has eroded backwards creating Fourth Canyon, which stretches 3 miles

NEW LAKE IN NAHANNI NATIONAL PARK
On or around March 1, 1997, the side of an unnamed mountain slid into the Clearwater Creek valley, blocking the drainage and creating an 11-mile (18-km) lake. This new dam was 10.5 miles (17 km) upstream from the confluence with the Nahanni. Due to the remoteness of the location, the phenomenon was not immediately noticed. As the waters accumulated, the earthen dam was breached and a torrential flood ensued. We had two groups on the river downstream from Clearwater Creek. Both reported a rise in the river's level, which seemed to be the highest in recorded history. One of the groups had to pack up camp around midnight just as its island campsite disappeared under the water. Fortunately both groups weathered the flood and now have dramatic stories to tell.

The initial extent of the lake in the flooded valley and the new water level when the waters receded following the bursting of the dam. A subsequent investigation by federal geologists resulted in the remaining dam being classified as permanent.

What was the cause of this calamity? Did global climate change cause enough permafrost to melt and create such a slump? It seems the answer may lie deeper within the earth's crust. Seismic records for the time period in question show a significant event of 3.8 on the Richter scale. Of course the first question is, Did the seismic activity cause the slide or did the landslide cause the seismic reading? Specialists indicate that the movement of tectonic plates which result in the seismic tremors are responsible for shaking the mountainside loose, causing the blockage.

The upside of this event is that the park now has a new lake, which people can explore. And there is also the visual evidence of dramatic geological change within our lifetime.

(5 km) downstream from the falls. Also known as Painted Canyon, its walls are adorned with wind-carved hoodoos and a collage of colors. In stark contrast to the technical rapids of the headwaters, the broad deep channel provides a roller-coaster ride of standing waves. Raft expeditions begin here, taking advantage of the fast water and avoiding the slow section above.

The four canyons have been numbered by travelers moving upstream, and so paddlers encounter them in reverse. Within Third Canyon you can scramble to the top of the narrow chasm known as "The Gate." Here

Grizzly is a species that may be seen on all of these rivers.

OPPOSITE PAGE:
Canoeing the flat meander-
ing river between
Rabbitkettle Lake and
Virginia Falls. The slick,
smooth surface betrays the
whitewater waiting below
the falls.

LEFT: *The Gate and Pulpit*
Rock dwarf the raft and
travelers, who float peace-
fully below.

the river squeezes to a third of its previous width and sneaks through a gap marked by the pinnacle of Pulpit Rock. A panoramic view of the canyon walls unfolds, punctuated by the 400-foot (130-m) tall spire below. Geologists tell us that at one time the gorge of the Gate did not exist and the river circumvented the existing chasm in an immense meander. A passageway eroded through the side of the canyon where the narrowest piece of wall existed between the looping channel, connecting the two portions of the river and circumventing the meander. A land bridge remained over the connecting passage and it eventually crumbled into the present gorge.

Second Canyon provides an impressive gateway to Deadmen Valley. It was here in 1905 that the headless bodies of prospecting brothers, Frank and Willie McLeod, were found. The men who discovered the dead brothers named the place of the last McLeod camp Headless Creek. Deadmen Valley was the name given to the surrounding mountain-ringed valley. To this day, the cause of the McLeods' death remains a mystery. The deep-cut canyons of Prairie Creek and Dry Canyon enter the valley, cutting through the Nahanni Plateau. The combined visual effect is stunning.

It feels sacrilegious to do anything but float through First Canyon. For this is the inner sanctum of the Nahanni and thus must be savored with respect and reverence. Pillars, flying buttresses, turrets, spires, and ramparts give a heraldic aspect to the twisting walls. The

Prairie Creek at its confluence with the Nahanni in Deadmen Valley.

black and gray stone is treeless except for the occasional black spruce clinging tenaciously to a fragile niche.

Over 3400 feet (1000 m) in height, First Canyon is one of the deepest river canyons on the continent. The walls of this canyon are steeper because they consist of harder dolomite rock, which is less susceptible to erosion.

One of the most spectacular campsites in the world lies in the depths of First Canyon. In the shadow of these cathedral cliffs stretches a broad sandy beach, almost a mile (1.6 km) long. Backed by tall cottonwoods, spruce, and piled high with driftwood, it is majestic in any weather. Clouds passing among the mountain palisades unite earth and sky. Dall's sheep wander the crags above. Moose or mountain caribou can often be seen fording the river.

Hundreds of sinkholes puncture the plateau above. Here lies another Nahanni superlative: the largest, most complex high-altitude karst system in the world. Rock towers, natural bridges and culverts, and eight major dry canyons provide dramatic evidence of the action of water on rock. Due to the lack of recent glaciation, these soft limestone features have survived the ages. In addition, over 200 cave entrances have been mapped in the canyon walls. In Grotte Valerie, more than 100 Dall's sheep skeletons have been found in a single cave. In order to preserve the cave's delicate environment, this area has been declared out of bounds to visitors.

One would expect the Nahanni to be more turbulent, given that it is a mountain river with a steep gradient. Its calm can be explained by the history of Glacial Lakes Nahanni and Tetcela. These were created at different times during the last Ice Age when the downstream end of the river was blocked by Laurentide ice. In First Canyon, Glacial Lake Nahanni filled twice over the course of time and was more than 1100 feet (360 m) deep. The smaller Glacial Lake Tetcela was 650 feet (200 m) deep. The Nahanni has not yet eroded the deposits of silt and clay left behind by the lakes above the original bedrock. Hence the river has a relatively smooth bottom.

Kraus Hotsprings signals the end of the canyons. While soaking in the natural sulfur springs, river travelers enjoy gazing into the mouth of the canyon and recounting tales of upriver adventure.

As it leaves the confines of the canyons, the river widens. The resulting braided channels are known as The Splits. With the use of binoculars, the watchful observer can spot The Sand Blowouts. These curious sandstone hoodoos lie between two peaks and have been sculpted by the wind as it funnels through the basin.

The Nahanni begins to meander as it approaches its junction with the Liard River and the Dene village of Nahanni Butte, the sole community on the river (population 97).

Naha Dehe is the name for Nahanni in the Dene language and refers to the river as well as the village. Artifacts found around nearby Chitu (Yohin Lake) indicate a human presence reaching back 9,000 to 10,000 years ago.

Whitespray Springs issues forth from the near vertical walls of First Canyon. Cool and crystal clear, the water is contained in massive reservoirs within the limestone. The process of water dissolving limestone creates Karst formations. The Nahanni Plateau above First Canyon is riddled with these features.

Oral history maintains that Naha Dehe (South Nahanni) was home to the Naha. As a mountain-dwelling people, they traveled the river using moose-hide boats. The Naha were considered by their neighbors to be a fierce people and had a reputation for attacking the lowlanders. Because of this the people of the lowlands seldom ventured above Nailicho (Virginia Falls). Archeology indicates they moved out of Naha Dehe by the 1880s. Oral history tells of an ambush by the lowlanders that annihilated the Naha. It is said that some Naha intermarried with the people of Naha Dehe (Nahanni Butte) and are recognized as such even today.

Paddling the slow flat meanders above the village, one might reminisce on Patterson's words in *Dangerous River*:

> *We had been allowed to live for a little time in a world apart, a lonely world of surpassing beauty, that has given us all things from somber magnificence of the canyons to the gay sunshine of those windswept uplands; from the quiet of the dry side canyons to the uproar of the broken waters—a land where men pass and the silence falls back into place behind them.*

As the title of his book indicates, it is a dangerous river; the greatest hazard is that you will fall in love with the regal river with the beautiful name and be drawn back to it repeatedly by its charm.

Land of the midnight sun. The June sky over Nahanni at 2:00 a.m.

CHAPTER 2

Alsek River (Yukon Territory, British Columbia, Alaska): World's Largest Bio Preserve

From the World Heritage Site plaque: Kluane National Park and Reserve and the adjoining Wrangell-St.Elias National Monument in Alaska were jointly nominated to the World Heritage List in 1979. Since that time, Glacier Bay National Park and Preserve and Tatshenshini-Alsek Park have been added to the site, creating the Kluane-Wrangell, St. Elias-Glacier Bay-Tatshenshini-Alsek World Heritage Site. The qualities that led to the initial nomination are: an unbroken, pristine natural system with a rich variety of vegetation patterns and ecosystems, a wealth of wildlife populations, including grizzly bears, Dall's sheep (the largest single concentration in the world), and a number of rare plant communities. They also contain the largest non-polar ice field in the world and some of the world's most spectacular glaciers.

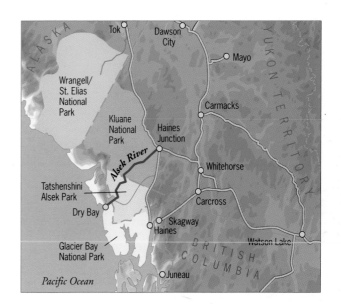

In the late 1980s the media was awash with references to the Tatshenshini River, due to a disputed mining project. If anything, the publicity understated the beauty and drama of the river. History dealt a curious hand with the lack of mention of another beautiful river only one valley over from the Tat, and into which it flows. The Alsek River has its origins only a short distance from the Tatshenshini, and while both are majestic, the difference between the two is dramatic. Because the

4:00 a.m. sunrise on Lowell Lake.

media campaign of the mine issue was fixated on the name Tatshenshini, the magnificent Alsek remains relatively unknown but much deserving of recognition.

The alpine origins of the Alsek begin with the confluence of the Dezadeash and Kaskawulsh Rivers in Kluane National Park. These two streams join to form the Alsek River. Surrounded by some of Canada's tallest mountain peaks, this broad glacial-carved valley within

~~~~~~

Kluane National Park is distinctly representative of high-altitude ecosystems. This remote and wild area has a dense population of grizzly bears. In fact, the grizzly population is so robust that it is the ongoing subject of biological study. The reports submitted by our guides form an important record that contributes to these studies.

The evidence of a recent geological event of grand proportion serves to further distinguish the Alsek. In the latter half of the 1800s the river was entirely bridged and blocked by a sudden surging movement of the Lowell Glacier, approximately 32 miles (50 km) downstream of its origin. The resulting lake behind the "ice dam," backed up over an area of hundreds of square miles, even flooding the current town site of Haines Junction. The ice plug remained for a few years until the river finally broached it. In a cataclysmic event the valley below was flushed by a flow of gargantuan proportion—a volume equivalent to the mighty Amazon. First Nations oral history tells of a village that was decimated by the floodwaters. The basin carved out by the glacier formed Lowell Lake. Today you see scarring and other effluvial remains that tell the story of the

Ariel view looking across the iceberg dotted Lowell Lake. Only a little longer than a century ago, the ice completely covered the lake, reaching the base of the mountain. The resulting dam flooded a vast region of the Yukon, including the present location of the village of Haines Junction.

monstrous hydrological event. Ripples like those you would see forming on a beach under the lapping waters can be seen on the land above the river. Only, these ripples are huge, their size a testament to the speed with which the massive flood drained. Another curious phenomenon is the granite "drop rocks" that litter the bank above the lake. These sharp-edged oddities differ distinctly from their rounded cousins that have been rolled in place by hydrological forces. Instead the drop rocks were embedded in glacier ice, which calved off as icebergs into the great flooded lake and then drifted with the wind. As they gradually melted, the bergs dropped

The rapids between Lowell Lake and Turnback Canyon sport to Class IV whitewater. The wildest of the rapids have a by-pass trail, for which travelers may opt.

〜〜〜〜〜〜〜〜〜〜〜〜〜〜〜〜

〜〜〜〜〜〜〜〜〜〜〜〜〜〜〜〜

Origin: Confluence of Dezadeash and Kaskawulsh Rivers, Kluane National Park, Yukon Territory
Length: 255 km (160 miles)
Drop: 555 m (1655 feet)
Completion: Dry Bay on the Gulf of Alaska
Unique Status: Flows through Kluane National Park, 10,000 sq. km Tatshenshini- Alsek Park, Glacier Bay National Park and Preserve, and adjacent to Wrangell St. Elias National Park. Designated a Canadian Heritage River in 1986.
Departure regulation system is in place to limit river trip embarkation to one trip per day. This ensures each visitor has the same chance of a wilderness experience.

Mount Vancouver rises above all else at 5,959 meters (15,699 feet) high.

their granite payload to the lake bottom, which is now riverbank.

The iceberg-dotted Lowell Lake is all that remains of the vast flood. Camping here, one can take the opportunity to hike up Goatherd Mountain for panoramic views of the ice fields, as well as some of the tallest peaks of the St. Elias Range: Kennedy, Alverstone and Hubbard. Mountain goats and Dall's sheep vie for your attention, and spectacularly lush flora fill your camera lens in the alpine meadows. Looking out over the lake, it is easy to follow the lines of the massive glacier and imagine it extending to the base of Goatherd. In those days you could have stepped off the mountain trail and onto the top of the glacier! Now the glacier calves icebergs into the lake, creating a serene and surreal setting through which one paddles to cross the lake. Most travelers agree that the combination is unlike anything they have witnessed before.

The mountains downstream of Lowell Lake crowd inwards, yielding narrow canyons. The water surges through with several distinct rapids and seemingly endless wave trains past an ever-changing vista. Deep within the heart of the St. Elias Mountains, the Tweedsmuir Glacier, the largest on the river, confronts the Alsek on the west side. To the east lies the base of Mount Blackadar. Acting like a huge funnel, they force the river down a narrow confine and crowd it into a deep gorge, appropriately known as Turnback Canyon. Downstream the river plunges through a 10-mile (16-km)

twisting series of horrendous rapids. Though this part of the river has been kayaked several times by extreme adventurers, it is considered unsafe for rafts.

For those rafting the river, the never-ending drama continues to unfold above the canyon. Here a helicopter can be summoned and everything—rafts, gear and people—is ferried on a spectacular flight over the glacier and canyon. The 360-degree view from the helicopter is a montage of rugged peaks and massive glaciers. Thanks to the deft skill of a mountain-trained pilot, you forget you are in a jet-propelled mechanical conveyance and feel as though you are hovering unaided above the magical setting. Once safely downstream, the rafts are inflated and rigged again, and the river expedition resumes.

Below the canyon, the river environment takes on a distinctly more lush setting. Thick alders and spruce crowd the valley and mountain slopes, with the exception of the Vern Ritchie and Battle Glaciers, which scrape the valleys. Not far below is the confluence of the Tatshenshini and Alsek Rivers. On the map, the two rivers join to create a wishbone-shaped valley. Here the two great rivers swell to stretch nearly three miles (5 km) wide, surging through braided channels that criss-cross the valley. The resulting union bears the name Alsek River and the river soon enters the state of Alaska and Glacier Bay National Park.

The Alsek cuts a giant bend which can be seen from space, and is encircled by peaks in a stunning

RIGHT: *The helicopter portage around Turnback Canyon. Here the Tweedsmuir Glacier narrows the Alsek River against the base of Mount Blackadar. A helicopter lifts the gear around the canyon. Then it returns for the travelers. From the air they get a bird's-eye view of the unnavigable canyon and the surrounding peaks and sprawling glaciers.*

OPPOSITE PAGE: *The highly glaciated coastal mountains, through which the Alsek and Tatshenshini flow, forming vital "green corridors." The valleys of these rivers form important links between the interior and the coast. This is critical for the health of flora and fauna populations and genetic diversity. Mount Logan is in the background: Canada's highest mountain.*

ABOVE: *Arctic tern in flight. These birds nest across the Arctic and can be found on all of the rivers from Alaska to Nunavut.*

OPPOSITE PAGE: *Alsek River sky.*

amphitheater of glacial ice and rock. The lush growth of the rock faces seems incongruous, juxtaposed against the harshness of the ice. The abundant foliage is a sign of the moist coastal climate that prevails here. The crystal-blue hues of Walker Glacier lie up ahead. It is a place where you can actually hike on the surface of the ancient ice and experience the unique environment of deep crevasses and jagged seracs and ice falls. Rivulets of meltwater converge on the surface, forming channels in the ice, only to drop through sculpted wells deep into the heart of the glacier. The extra half-mile you now have to hike to reach the glacier, compared with 15 years ago, is a stark reminder of the shrinking of the planet's glaciers.

As you float downstream you can see more than 20 glaciers. Where the Alsek and Grand Plateau Glaciers come together at the river they form an eight-mile-wide (13 km) face of ice. Spectacular camping is enjoyed at Alsek Lake, which was formed by the gouging action of the glaciers, resulting in the largest lake in Glacier Bay National Park. The old terminal moraine, pushed up by the toe of the glacier before it receded, forms a spit of land, blocking the lake from much of the river. The only thing that breaks the mystical spell of the iceberg-filled lake with the mountain backdrop is the frequent explosive crescendos of calving glaciers which spawn multi-ton icebergs. Overseeing the phenomenon is Mount Fairweather whose ice-clad summit soars over 15,000 feet (4572 m) above the lake.

Enjoying and exploring the lake is a delight for all the senses. The final reach of the stately river is from Alsek Lake to Dry Bay on the Gulf of Alaska. At the tiny commercial fishing enclave, just upstream of the estuary in the gulf, itinerant fishers continue to pursue a commercial fishery in the face of dropping salmon stocks. Bush planes are able to land here. They carry river travelers back to their quotidian world with a load of memories and recollections of the majestic Alsek.

CHAPTER 3

Tatshenshini (Yukon Territory, Alaska): Ice Age River

"The Tatshenshini-Alsek is one of the most magnificent river systems on earth, flowing through one of the world's most pristine wilderness areas. The region is prime habitat for large mammals including the grizzly, the rare glacier bear, moose, wolf, mountain goat and Dall sheep, and birds such as the bald eagle, peregrine falcon and trumpeter swan. It is a place of exceptional quality and environmental significance. The Tatshenshini-Alsek features tremendous biological diversity and overwhelming natural beauty, which should be protected and preserved for future generations."
—FORMER UNITED STATES VICE PRESIDENT AL GORE

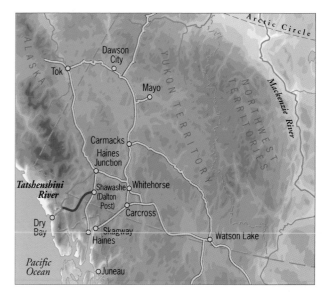

The Tatshenshini emerged from obscurity in the late 1980s. Plans for a small gold mine in the heart of the roadless region changed to a large copper mine, requiring a road, bridges, and massive tailings ponds. In this area the mountains are still growing, making it more seismically unstable than the San Andreas Fault of California. The plan to have the acidic waters of the tailings perched above a major salmon river sparked international concern. The Tatshenshini-Alsek was put at the top of the list of the 10 most endangered rivers in America. As a result, Tatshenshini Alsek Park was formed and the region now comprises the heart of the largest biological preserve in the world without a mine or roads.

The Alsek and Grand Plateau Glaciers carved out a basin and pushed up a terminal moraine. As they have receded, the basin has filled with water, forming Alsek Lake. The terminal moraine separates most of the lake from the river and provides scenic camping for river travelers. Floating in a raft among the icebergs is a surreal experience.

The Tatshenshini River begins as only a tiny trickle amid the alpine meadows of the Chilkat Summit. This

Origin: Chilkat Summit

Length: 152 miles (245 km)

Drop: 1950 feet (650 m)

Completion: Confluence with the Alsek River (rafters continue on, via the Alsek River, to Dry Bay on the Gulf of Alaska.)

Unique Status: Flows through 3860-square-mile (10,000-sq.-km) Tatshenshini Alsek Park adjacent to Kluane National Park, Glacier Bay National Park and Reserve and Wrangell St Elias National Park.
A departure regulation system is in place to limit river trip embarkation to one trip per day. This ensures each visitor has the same chance of a wilderness experience.

RIGHT: *Red Columbine.*

OPPOSITE PAGE:
Camping on Alsek Lake. The presence of the icebergs in the warm maritime climate makes for an exotic setting.

burgeoning rivulet eventually swells to more than half a mile (about one km) in breadth. At its confluence with the Alsek River, the two rivers rival the largest drainages on the continent. Together they form a vital green cor-

ridor, between the interior and coast, through the highly glaciated and rugged peaks of the St. Elias Range and coastal mountains. Below the spectacular peaks, the broad lush valley is home to large populations of grizzlies, bald eagles, moose, wolves and other animals. These qualities have earned the river a reputation as a coveted destination. Visitors are often torn between the choice of beginning their trip on the Tatshenshini or the Alsek. Those who have experienced both say you must keep each of them on your list.

Cavorting with whitewater abandon from the alpine reaches, the Tatshenshini meets Klukshu Creek at the historic Southern Tuchone village of Shawashee. Raft expeditions launch at this site, as the last road access to the river is here. For countless generations, First Nations families have gathered here to capture spawning salmon which leave the Tatshenshini for Klukshu Creek.

Farther up the creek, at the village of Klukshu, one can still witness the use of traditional fish traps and smokehouses which have provided sustenance for thousands of years.

Below the Klukshu confluence, the river rushes into a canyon rift in the Squanga Range. The Class IV whitewater creates a barrier for all but expedition rafts and a handful of expert canoeists and kayakers. Foaming holes, submerged rocks, and slick drops spell whitewater paradise. Abrupt bends below rock walls and narrow routes through boulder-strewn chutes demand the full attention from the river guides piloting the craft.

After 19 miles (30 km), as though it is resting for more to come, the Tatshenshini enters a calmer section. Here it meanders through green moose meadows under the watchful eyes of bald eagles. Immersed in

Back at the turn of the last century, a man named Jack Dalton built a trading post here at Shawashee. He had the idea of charging a toll to other traders heading inland for the use of his road (which happened to follow the First Nations trails). He was also known for issuing his own currency in exchange for furs. He traded poker chips that could be redeemed for goods at his post. This may have been the first and most far-flung experiment with coupons.

dense alder and willow trees, belted kingfishers, beavers and spawning salmon compete for attention. The close curtain of thick foliage hides the visual treasure that lies ahead. After a day of weaving through this verdant area, the river cascades into the open, broad U-shaped valley with a sudden swoosh and reveals the towering St. Elias Range.

The Tatshenshini increases in volume and speed as it courses back and forth through braided channels across the broad, glacially carved valley. The gradient is steep and the river extremely swift. Turbulent boils form where channels converge among the braids. The large rafts mask the power of the hydraulics, which would instantly overturn a smaller craft. Amazingly, the river

Alpine hiking above Tatshenshini. The effort can be rewarded with sightings of mountain goats and Dall's sheep. Hikes must be strategically planned so that they take advantage of existing trails through the thick coastal growth.

Deep in the heart of the Tatshenshini, in the summer of 1999, an age-old secret of the highly glaciated Coast Range was uncovered. On the edge of a glacier, three hunters made a spectacular archeological discovery. Drawn to some unusual pieces of wood, the men spotted something that looked like a mitten. Upon closer examination it appeared to be part of a body beneath the surface of the ice. They later reported that a skeletal pelvic structure was "lying on its front in the thin ice and covered with dark brown leather clothing and what appeared to be a backpack." Through the ice, they could see that there was skin and muscle tissue intact. Realizing that they had stumbled upon something remarkable, they carefully recorded the location of the body and made the two-day hike out to civilization to announce their discovery. It was immediately apparent to authorities that this was a major archaeological find. Overnight the discovery attracted international attention.

The ancient person was presumed to be of First Nations ancestry and as such his remains were given a name: Kwaday Dan Sinchi— Southern Tuchone for "long ago person found." The lower torso was discovered first. Further melting yielded a spruce root hat, gopher-skin robe, an unidentified tool in a pouch and a spear-throwing device known as an Atlatl. The timing of this find was perfect. In a short while,

remains less rough than its steep gradient would seem to dictate. This is because a gravel-and sediment-filled bed smoothes the river bottom, keeping the descent from becoming an unnavigable maelstrom.

At one point, a narrow constriction belies the dynamic, ever changing nature of the valley. This constriction was caused by a massive landslide from the overlooking mountain, this feature is only 20 years old! The resulting rapids formed by the constriction bear the moniker Monkey Wrench Rapids. It was here in the mid 1980s that river guides spotted orange flagging tape. The survey tape marked the location of a future bridge that would cross the river, allowing the creation of a road through the heart of the Tatshenshini to service the proposed copper mine. In the spirit of an early environmental activist, Edward Abbey, the guides removed the tape, throwing a "monkey wrench" as it were, into the bridge plans. Hence the rapids' name.

Vast alluvial fans of rounded rock debris spread out where they have issued from side canyons. At times in their ongoing evolution, these fans have spilled into the valley, constricting the river. This is an ongoing process *the remains would have lost the refrigerating protection of the ice and succumbed to scavengers and the elements. Normally, the organic components of skin, sinew, roots and human flesh would have disintegrated soon after the death. In this case, destiny preserved them for our generation to discover. The Champagne and Aishihik First Nations people, for whom this region is home, supported forensic examination of the remains. The examination revealed that the ancient person had died over 500 years ago. In a traditional ceremony the descendants of this person finally put his remains to rest.*

Many things have since been learned from the studies of the remains. One mysterious question was raised by the 500-year-old tool, which consisted of a wooden handle with a small piece of iron inserted to form an awl or pick. How did this metal find its way into the heart of the Tatshenshini, before Columbus arrived and hundreds of years before the First Nations people had contact with European culture? It is thought that the iron may have originated as a spike in a piece of timber that washed ashore on the west coast of Alaska. Oral tradition tells of such finds before contact with whites. The spike would have been extracted, perhaps by burning or cutting. The discovery of this tool confirms that there was movement of people and goods between the coast and interior before the arrival of Europeans.

and the river fights back by cutting away at the intrusion. As you drift past these cut faces, they appear markedly straight and sharp, surgically incised, leaving impossibly steep-faced gravel banks. These banks would slump to a shallower incline if not for the continuous erosion of the river—further evidence that the process is ongoing. In contrast to the translucent green waters of the upper canyon, here the river takes on the color of chocolate milk, with a heavy burden of glacial silt.

A day-long hike allows you to take in stunning alpine beauty. Hiking opportunities in the rich coastal ranges are rewarding, but they must be strategically planned. The dense coastal rain forest of willow and alder is impenetrably thick, except where game trails exist. The alpine area is home to mountain goats and Dall's sheep, as well as Merlins, American kestrels and golden eagles, among other creatures. You never seem to have enough film on these hikes to capture these sights.

As the Tatshenshini spills toward the confluence with the Alsek River, the mountain slopes above take on the verdant lushness of alders and fuscia fireweed, which carpets all but the steepest rocky crags. The confluence

OPPOSITE PAGE:
Tatshenshini camp with the snow-capped St. Elias Range in the background.

LEFT: *Hiking on Walker Glacier. The toe of this glacier has receded nearly half a mile in the last decade.*

is a vast sprawling region dotted with islands and gravel bars. Travelers who scan the shores with binoculars are often rewarded with the sighting of grizzlies.

Alpine glaciers become evident in the peaks, and

In the late 1800s John Muir was lured northward from California to the coast of Alaska to explore and learn about the massive glaciers that poured down from the mountains to the coast. Upon his arrival in Glacier Bay, Alaska, he recorded this observation: "About noon we discovered the first of the great glaciers...Its lofty blue cliffs, looming through the draggled skirts of the clouds, gave a tremendous impression of savage power, while the roar of the new-born icebergs thickened and emphasized the general roar of the storm."

sprawling, sparkling valley glaciers stretch down toward the river. As the Tatshenshini joins the already mighty Alsek, the two cut through the coastal ranges. So entwined are these two great rivers that river travelers think of them as a single entity. In truth, the Tatshenshini surrenders its name and turns over its load of silt, sediment, and a small number of travelers to continue to the Gulf of Alaska, via the majestic Alsek.

Glacial Primer—Rivers of Ice

To the uninitiated, glaciers are an enigma. These sprawling white masses of ice that snake through mountain peaks, dominate high places, and shape the land beneath, forever changing the mountain landscape—are intimidating and enchanting to the viewer. To demystify the phenomenon, a description of how icebergs originated follows. It is based on the explanation river guide Martha Taylor offers her guests as they hike upon Walker Glacier.

Glaciers first appeared 83 million years after the earth began cooling following the Pliocene epoch. Snow started to accumulate over the northern portions of the globe and even in mid latitudes. The reasons for this accumulation are debated but the results are evident even today. As the snow amassed, it exerted pressure on the underlying layers. At great depths the fresh snow compressed into a granular form called firn. Over time and with increased pressure of the building snow mass above, the firn became so compressed that it turned into glacial ice. Thus were created the vast continental glaciers that slowly moved over the mountain ranges of the world. This geological era is known as the Pleistocene epoch of the Quaternary period and it encompasses the last 1.87 million years. The world's climate has changed since that time. Today, most glaciers we encounter are relegated to the high jagged mountains of the world.

Glaciers are in a constant state of motion—they are either advancing or retreating. As the snow accumulates on the upper portion of the glacier it exerts pressure on the snow and ice below, causing it to flow, albeit at a pace not visible to the human eye. When the rate of melting exceeds the rate of accumulating snow, the glacier retreats. The rate of retreat can be measured by noting the distance between succeeding terminal moraines (ridges of glacial deposits). Great Glacier Lake on the Stikine River is cut off from the river by one of the Great Glacier's terminal moraines. This moraine acts as a damn and keeps the lake from flooding into the river. If a glacier is retreating very rapidly, there is no distinct terminal moraine. Instead, there is a more general ground moraine.

Virtually every mountain range has been affected by glaciers. While widening river valleys into broad "U" shapes, they create high narrow ridges called aretes, pyramid-shaped peaks termed horns, and scooped-out alpine basins named cirques. The power of the ice as it flows over the mountain's surface shapes the land over which it passes and picks up the ground material, which is carried on by the glacier. Most people do not realize that the underlying stone is ground away by particulate matter in the meltwater that runs between the ice and the ground or by rocks carried by the glacier. It is not actually carved by the ice.

A close-up view of glaciers reveals dark lines of rubble running down the middles or edges. The middle ridges, known as medial moraines, mark the joining of two separate glaciers. Lateral moraines mark the edges where melt water from the glacier dumps the rock material it is carrying.

The Alsek, Tatshenshini, and Stikine Rivers offer breathtaking views of hundreds of glaciers. These rivers promise "up close" views of icebergs—both Alsek Lake on the Tatshenshini and Great Glacier Lake on the Stikine contain icebergs. Here, the toes of the glaciers end in a body of water where ice movement and fracturing causes enormous, multi-tonne slabs of ice to fall off the face of the glacier in a noisy crescendo and plunge into the water. This process of giving birth to these icebergs is appropriately termed calving. The resulting iceberg floats silently until melting upsets its balance, causing it to roll in an explosive action, which sends large rolling waves out into the lake. John Muir described a calving glacier as "an array of jagged spires [and] battlements, of many shades of blue, from pale shimmering, limpid tones in the crevasses and hollows, to the most startling, chilling, almost shrieking vitriol blue on the plain mural spaces from which bergs had just been discharged." The blue color is a result of the dense ice molecules reflecting blue waves of light.

The Walker Glacier on the Tatshenshini provides visitors with an opportunity to hike on its surface. Much of this glacier is an interrupted array of jagged ice known as an icefall. Here the underlying ground is too steep for the overriding ice to flow smoothly. The stresses forced on the upper ice are so great that the ice opens up into a series of crevasses that form the steps of the icefall. These deep slots must be carefully tread on by travelers.

CHAPTER 4

Firth River (Ivvavik National Park Yukon Territory): Porcupine Caribou Herd

The Northern Yukon is an arctic and sub-arctic wilderness of incredible beauty, a rich and varied ecosystem: nine million acres of land and animals…a place of contrasts, of an explosively productive but brief summer and of a long hard winter, of rugged mountains and stark plains. Its teeming marshes and shore lands give it a beauty equaled by few other places on Earth.

—JUSTICE THOMAS BERGER IN HIS 1977 REPORT *NORTHERN FRONTIER, NORTHERN HOMELAND*, WHICH CALLED FOR A 10-YEAR MORATORIUM ON A MACKENZIE VALLEY PIPELINE

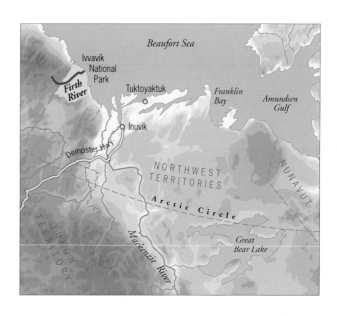

Mountains, canyons, tundra, and Arctic coast—the Firth River has it all. Ivvavik National Park, through which the river flows, is truly a marvel of diversity and a tantalizing collection of contrasting and intriguing features. Parks Canada recognizes this portion of the Yukon as "an area of spectacular scenery and exceptional ecological significance."

River travelers set out on their adventure from the remote frontier community of Inuvik, a town established in 1955 as a supply base for Beaufort Sea petroleum exploration. The name of the town means "place of humans" in the Inuvialuit language. Winging westward in a Twin Otter aircraft, the flight passes over the biologically rich maze of waterways of the Mackenzie River delta. Farther on, it enters into a series of undulating and predominantly treeless mountain ranges intersected by meandering river courses. Toward the coast, well-developed shrub tundra vegetation is present in wetter areas. This is typical of the Yukon's North Slope, so named because the plain of the northern Yukon coastline gently slopes toward the Beaufort Sea. The British, Barn, and northern Richardson Mountains form a rugged barrier between

The canyon of the Firth River slashes the tableland of the tundra.

Origin: British Mountains on the border of Alaska and the Yukon Territory

Length: 94 Miles (150 kilometers)

Drop: 1500 feet (460 meters)

Completion: Beaufort Sea near Herschel Island

Unique Status: Flows through Ivvavik National Park Departure regulation system ensures each visitor has the same chance of a wilderness experience.

Walking along Nunaluk Spit on the Beaufort Sea at 2:00 a.m.

the coastal plains and the Old Crow Flats to the south. The coastal plain is rich in wetlands, but contains an underlayer of permafrost 300 feet (100 m) thick. A thin surface layer thaws each summer, but the underlying frozen ground prevents drainage and causes standing water to gather in depressions. Most of the ground is wet to the touch through the summer. These rich wetlands display permafrost features, the most common being "patterned ground." A good example of this phenomenon is the honeycomb-like tundra polygons. These multi-sided, raised clumps of clay and vegetation are heaved up by frost and bordered by troughs. Where drainage is slightly better, vast expanses of cotton grass bloom amid the tussocks. In late June and July delicate wildflowers carpet the tundra and hillsides with a palette of color.

The flight destination is Margaret Lake, 160 miles (255 km) from Inuvik, where the gravel-bedded Firth River flows through an open valley. Craggy limestone peaks mark gently sloping velvety green hillsides. Upstream, the Firth River originates in the British Mountains of the Brooks Range of Alaska. Margaret Lake lies at 1,500 ft (460 m) above sea level; pockets of small spruce trees dot the valley bottom, while the slopes are covered with dry tundra vegetation. This is the extreme edge of the tree line where most spruce must "clone" to reproduce.

Below Margaret Lake, the Firth is swift and shallow with a steep gradient that foreshadows the wild Class IV whitewater below. Flowing through the broad valley, the river soon enters a 25-mile-long (40-kilometer), 10,000-year-old canyon. The gorge is 45 to 60 feet (15–20 m) deep and marks the western boundary of glaciation on the Yukon North Slope. Gyrfalcons, peregrines, golden eagles, and other birds of prey nest along the canyon walls. As one scans the cliffs, one sees vertical streaks of lichen on the steep rock, which often signals the existence of raptor nests. These birds have nested in clefts in the cliffs for thousands of years, thus the steady supply of rich bird droppings. Over time, these droppings have nourished the slowly growing lichen. Long sets of exciting rapids with boulders, ledges, and holes, make for an exhilarating raft ride.

Hiking opportunities abound along the river's course. As one walks along the rolling ridges, one finds frequent evidence of the migrating caribou. Hoof prints from the annual migration, antlers, bone and the floating hair from the 150,000-strong herd swimming the river serve as evidence of the passing of the Porcupine caribou herd. It is a frequent reminder that this land is home to people of a caribou culture. Over the centuries, the animal has represented an essential core to human survival. The caribou is a versatile provider. Meat, hides for clothing and shelter, bone for tools, sinews for sewing, and fat for light and heat, are central to the First Nation's culture.

Above the Firth's canyons, the remnants of caribou fences can be found. These simple features of rock were

positioned to encourage the caribou to move into strategic locations where the hunters could kill them using spears or bows and arrows. The most recent hunters of caribou, the Inuvialuit, have relied on the animals for sustenance for hundreds of years. While most Inuvialuit now live in nearby communities such as Aklavik, Tuktoyaktuk, and Inuvik, many regularly return to the North Slope to hunt and also fish. They still use their traditional gathering places in the mountains along the coast to preserve their culture and educate their families.

The river action remains captivating for the traveler. As it leaves the canyon reaches, the Firth spills out onto coastal tundra plains. To the east, a natural spire known as Engistciak, rises abruptly from the flat lands. Evidence of other cultures remains at the base of the outcrop. The elevated promontory has long been an important lookout point for First Nations hunters seeking game. An ancient fire pit and bone shards can be found at its base, revealing evidence of 5,000 years of occupation by nine different cultures. Sitting atop Engistciak, you can cast your gaze inland to get an uninterrupted view of the mountains, or you can look to the coast and out to the ocean. If you look down you can see where raptors nest on the cliff, taking advantage of the strategic rise. All of this drives home the relationship of the hunter-gatherer and the land.

The Firth travels through a maze of delta braids before entering a lagoon region sheltered by Nunaluk Spit. The beaches and islands at the mouth of the Firth are being constantly eroded and reformed by currents and winds. The delta formation, composed of channels, lakes, and ponds, is created from alluvial silt carried by the river from the mountaintops. Gravel beaches dominate the area and are dotted by driftwood from the Mackenzie River. These unique habitats are very important areas of nesting, staging, and refuge for shorebirds, seabirds, and sea ducks, which are drawn by the long hours of summer daylight and abundant insects. They use the coastal wetlands, spits, and small islands for feeding, nesting, and as safe places to molt.

During the spring and summer, many species of young fish use the warm, rich lagoons as a place to feed and grow. Arctic grayling, dolly varden and char use the upper reaches to spawn and over-winter. Others go out to sea before the winter's ice reclaims the brackish waters.

Nunaluk Spit is a broad expanse of gravel, washed by the ocean. It lies at the edge of the lagoons, offering enough flat beach on which to land a Twin Otter. Camping on the spit allows one to enjoy the coastal environment. From here, on the homeward flight, river travelers can fly a short distance to Herschel Island, known as *Qikiqtaruk* by the Inuvialuit. This island dominates the outlying edge of the Beaufort Sea. It was formed as glaciers from under the mainland thrust marine sediments up before the Laurentide ice sheet melted approximately 10,000 years ago. Between 1890 and 1907 commercial whaling fleets over-wintered at

the east end of the island in Pauline Cove. Now a National Historic Site. It was the sheltered waters of the cove that lured the whaling companies to over-winter. As many as 2,000 Caucasian and Inuit men and their ships would remain here until spring. Because of this the Northwest Mounted Police maintained a post on the

Tuktu, the Inuvialuit name for caribou, form an essential link between human survival and the North Slope natural environment. Masses of caribou trek to the North Slope from their wintering grounds south of the Porcupine River in early spring. In early June pregnant females congregate to give birth in early June west of the Firth River along the foothills of the British Mountains and in Alaska's Arctic National Wildlife Refuge. This barren-ground caribou herd of nearly 150,000 animals ranges over 250,000 square kilometers.

Ten animals of the Porcupine caribou herd are radio-collared and tracked by satellite. You can monitor their progress on a web site linked to the Firth River itinerary on www.nahanni.com, an amazing feature that records a remarkable phenomenon. The updating of the map locations is always delayed by one month in order to prevent hunters from using the modern technology to track the herd.

island and it was on a patrol from here that the fateful "Lost Patrol" of the Wind River originated (see chapter 6). The island was designated a Territorial Park by the Yukon Government several years ago in an effort to protect its unique natural and cultural history. A number of

Looking inland from the isolated spire of Engigstciak. This promontory has served as a strategic gathering point for people over the millennia.

LEFT: *Running "Sheep Slot" in the Firth River canyon. The Firth boasts Class IV whitewater and the canyon provides steady excitement for several days.*

OPPOSITE PAGE: *The coastal plains of the Firth River.*

~~~~~~~~~~~~~~~

~~~~~~~~~~~~~~~

the old buildings and gravesites are still standing. At 2:00 a.m. in July, the orb of light hanging in the sky is not the moon but the sun! The low-angle rays cast a glow on the land, bringing out radiant colors.

Herschel Island supports a rich diversity of wildlife. Black guillemots can be seen diving for herring. Muskox, grizzly, arctic and red fox, and caribou inhabit the island, and the warm nutrient-rich waters support both anadromous fish that can live in fresh and salt water, as well as marine fish and ringed and bearded seals, Beluga and bowhead whales. In the springtime, seabirds and waterfowl gather at early open water leads. In summer, the island supports North America's most dense breeding populations of rough-legged hawks.

Flying back toward Inuvik from Herschel Island, the dramatic view of this land where the mountains of North America meet the Arctic Ocean provides a fitting end to a fascinating journey through a wild and remote landscape.

Caribou—Buoyant River Swimmers

You may see one caribou silhouetted as a solitary figure on the horizon or 40,000 migrating across the river in front of you. In either case you will be entranced.

On many of our northern river expeditions we have had the opportunity to view caribou. These well-adapted creatures have roamed the tundra and provided sustenance to the land's inhabitants for thousands of years. They may be found from the tundra of the high arctic to the southern limit of the boreal forest, as far west as the coastal mountains and rain forests and east to the craggy shores of the Atlantic Ocean. Many significant archeological sites have been found at places that intercept the migratory patterns of these animals, indicating a long-standing relationship with humankind.

Caribou are members of the deer family. We often speak of them as either barren-ground or woodland caribou. The barren-ground species inhabits land from Hudson Bay to the Mackenzie River. Within this first species, there are five main herds and some smaller ones. Each is named for the region in which it calves. The Bathurst herd is named for Bathurst Inlet and is the most accessible herd to people because the southern edge of its range encompasses the city of Yellowknife. The Bluenose herd is named after Bluenose Lake; the Beverly after Beverly Lake in the Thelon Game Sanctuary; the Porcupine for the River of the same name in the northern Yukon and Alaska; and the Kaminuriak herd's namesake is Kaminuriak Lake just west of Hudson Bay.

The three northern subspecies are: Grant's caribou, woodland caribou and Peary caribou. The Porcupine herd of northern Yukon and northeastern Alaska are Grant's Caribou. Woodland caribou occur throughout Canada except in New Brunswick, Nova Scotia, and Prince Edward Island. They favor boreal forests and mountainous regions. Peary caribou are confined entirely to Canada's Arctic islands.

An often-asked question regards the relationship between caribou and reindeer. The fabled sleigh-pulling animals belong to the same species as caribou. However,

In addition to the caribou, wolves, grizzly bears, wolverines, moose and muskoxen are found in the variety of habitats in the northern mountains. Dall's sheep are the Yukon's most northernmost and isolated population.

they have shorter legs and a wider back. In northern Europe and Asia they have been domesticated for centuries. In the late 1890s, they were brought over to North America, and the reindeer that now inhabit the Northwest Territories are descendants of this herd. The visual similarity is so great that a Canadian court case declared it was unreasonable to expect a hunter to be able to distinguish reindeer from caribou.

As year-round foragers, the caribou must rely upon their sense of smell in winter to detect food through deep snow. Employing broad hooves, they dig to uncover hidden treasures. Lichen forms the bulk of their diet in the winter. In the summer this is replaced by new, more appetizing plant growth. Fungi is added to the diet in the fall.

Caribou eat while walking and as a result the damage sustained by the fragile plants they favor is reduced. Their way of eating also prevents over-harvesting of one area.

In their perpetual state of movement, the caribou frequently cross bodies of water. During the summer months this requires swimming. The caribou's hollow hair structure renders the animal extremely buoyant, which assists the caribou in water crossings. As they swim, they appear to float unusually high in the water. The water crossings are a time of great hazard for the animals. The danger starts before they reach the water. Shrubs thrive at the river's edge and provide excellent cover for wolves waiting to ambush. For this reason, the caribou approach river crossings very cautiously. The typical behavior upon reaching a river is for the front runners to slow and begin stationary grazing before nearing the shrubs. Soon, the numbers build up and at some point of critical mass, the animals charge down through the brush. This instinctive strategy underlies the fact that there is safety in numbers. On rivers like the Firth, the actual hydraulics of the river can create further difficulties for the caribou. In 2002, the unusually late spring melt of snow and ice yielded unusually high and fast water when the caribou arrived. This caused the animals to be carried farther down river during the crossing. Males with large antlers were particularly disadvantaged. Their heavy headgear was easily caught in the turbulent wave action, and they subsequently

RIGHT: *Firth River.*

OPPOSITE PAGE: *Caribou of the Porcupine Herd.*

A historic building on Herschel Island. At the turn of the century, the small island was home to over-wintering whaling fleets with as many as 2,000 men. The nesting boxes on the roof are home to Black Guillemots. The island is a Yukon Territorial Park in the Beaufort Sea. Herschel Island, known as Qikiqtaruk *by the Inuvialuit, was formed as glaciers from the mainland thrust marine sediments up before the Laurentide ice sheet melted.*

drowned. Following this migration, a pilot spotted 18 grizzlies feeding on carcasses within the canyon.

Traditional caribou hunters use every part of the animal. The hide is prized for warm clothing due to its superior insulative properties. The hair is structured in a network of honeycomb-shaped cells that are able to trap pockets of air. The individual hairs are densely packed together, enhancing the effect. Ice and snow that build up on the fur can be beaten off easily with wooden or bone "beaters."

Every piece of caribou flesh is edible, and even the fermented stomach contents are consumed. Considered a delicacy by the hunters, the contents are rich in plant nutrients required to stay healthy in an environment where plant life is not always available.

Bones are employed for scrapers, awls, knives, and other implements. The clicking sound made as a herd travels is thought to be caused by the articulation of the animals' ankle joints.

It is a happy coincidence that caribou are curious. As a result there is little sport in hunting them. They will often approach a hunter out of curiosity and show little fear of him. They have been referred to as "cattle of the barrens."

Even today caribou are, in essence, the life blood of many native people. James Pokiak, who guides our Horton River expedition, requires approximately 20 caribou per year to feed his family. Both the meat and the hides are essential to traditional lifestyle and survival in the Arctic.

A recent success story is the growth of the 40 Mile caribou herd, which migrates between Alaska and central Yukon. Biologists estimated that in the 1920s the herd numbered nearly 500,000. Riverboat captains on the Yukon River told stories of caribou so dense in numbers that they stopped the boats for days for fear of catching them in the paddle wheels. The population dropped precipitously to 10,000 in the '40s and '50s. This was mostly as a result of indiscriminate hunting caused by the pressures of access created by the war-time construction of the Alcan Highway. During this time, the migratory range shrunk, and the animals did not cross into the Yukon. The herd's recent recovery follows years of planning and some controversial predator controls. It is hoped that the numbers will reach 100,000 within a few decades. While the herd's growth is rare good news, it is sad that it is requiring human intervention to bring its numbers back to sustainable levels.

Biologists estimate that the NWT and Nunavut have 1,310,000 caribou. This is one for every square mile (2.6 sq. km). Put otherwise, it means there are 21 times more caribou in the area than people!

Crocus beneath the midnight sun. The fine hairs of the flower serve to create a sheath of still air around the petals, thereby elevating the temperature inside. Flowers of the arctic tundra employ a variety of strategies to make the most of a short, intense growing season.

CHAPTER 5

Snake River (Yukon Territory): Mountain Majesty—Untouched and Pristine

The resources of the country from my own personal observations are extremely good. Large animals, both moose and reindeer [actually caribou], are in the greatest abundance, especially in the upper parts of the river, which has not been much hunted. The river in summer abounds in excellent fish and the lakes in the fall and winter produce plenty for the support of an establishment.
—HUDSON BAY EXPLORER JOHN BELL IN 1839 UPON RETURNING FROM HIS EXPLORATION OF THE SNAKE RIVER REGION OF THE YUKON.

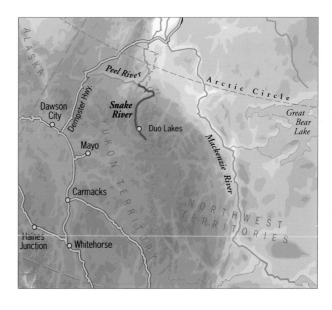

It is a stroke of luck that the Yukon's Snake River remains undeveloped and pristine. Remoteness from roads has, so far, protected the area's resources from commercial interests. John Bell's observations were more accurate than he could have known. Not only is the region rich in natural resources, it also has coveted mineral deposits. In modern times, there is a tension between the health of the area's surface richness and access to the richness below. Unfortunately, the road access that potential future mining companies would require to exploit the minerals would violate the pristine state that allows the abundant flora and fauna to thrive.

The flow of raft travelers on the river is low due to the complications of gaining access to it. A combination of floatplanes and helicopters is required to access the Snake with a raft. However, these elaborate travel arrangements result in a payoff—from the air there are exhilarating views and photo opportunities before you embark on the river. These access-related challenges, on the plus side, though, have rendered the Snake-Wind River region as one of the largest pristine places outside of park protected areas. The barrier of distance and the difficulty of accessing the area will not preserve it forever. Currently efforts are being

Lively whitewater, great hiking, and spectacular scenery make the Snake River a canoeist's paradise.

〰〰〰〰〰〰〰〰〰〰〰〰〰〰〰〰〰

〰〰〰〰〰〰〰〰〰〰

Origin: Werneke Mountains of
the Bonnet Plume range (near
Duo Lakes)

Length: 188 miles (300 km)

Drop: 2400 feet (800 m)

Completion: Confluence with
the Peel River

Unique Status: Currently a
candidate of a proposed
protected-areas strategy in
the Yukon

*Hiking in the Mount
MacDonald Range.*

made to ensure ongoing preservation through the
Yukon Protected Areas Strategy but the changing
winds of politics make the outcome of this strategy
uncertain. The Yukon chapter of the Canadian Parks
and Wilderness Society is working hard to see it
through and is an ongoing source of information on
the status of the process.

Dropping nearly 1,000 feet to the confluence with
the Peel River, the Snake is a challenging whitewater
river, suitable for rafting or for experienced whitewater
canoeists.

The river originates in the majestic Werneke
Mountains near Duo Lakes, where it is a shallow,
gravely stream. After portaging the short distance from
the lakes to the river, canoeists spend a day wading and

*John Bell was one of the earliest white explor-
ers to the area and was in the employ of the
Hudson's Bay Company. In the summer of
1839, he journeyed up the Snake, mistakenly
believing it was the headwaters of the Peel
River. So impressed was he with the abundance
of wildlife in the region that he recommended
the establishment of Fort McPherson on the
lower Peel. Bell may have been mistaken with
his geography, but he recognized a good thing
when he saw it!*

lining canoes downstream at the end of a rope until the
channel deepens and the real fun begins. Raft groups
"sling" their loads beneath a helicopter to the vicinity of
Reptile Creek. The odd name refers to the abundance of
fossils found among the rocks in the creek bed. Here
spectacular hiking abounds and the river channel is deep
enough to accommodate the expedition rafts.

Short canyon stretches punctuate the trip with
excitement. The ever-changing vista from the river is
only second to the expansive panoramas that can be
viewed on hikes to the overlooking mountain ridges.
Hiking into the alpine reaches is attractive on the Snake
as there is little bush to negotiate between the river and
the high country.

Watchful river travelers scanning the mountain
slopes will see Dall's sheep gracing the crags where pred-
ators will not tread. Beginning at lower elevations in the
spring, they forage on plants and move higher as the
greening of the grasses and sedges moves up the hillsides. The lambs stay close to the mothers in nursery
herds while the rams roam in bachelor herds.

As the Snake River leaves the sedimentary Werneke
Mountains of the Bonnet Plume Range, it flows north
into the Peel River Plateau. Here the topography
changes. High, rising banks are home to peregrine falcons, which bullet overhead. About one-quarter of the
Yukon's 200 breeding peregrine falcons make their
home on the Peel. Nearly obliterated by pesticides in the
1960s, they are making a strong comeback. Catching

sight of a swooping peregrine snatching a bird in a lightning dive is a spectacle one never forgets.

As one nears the Peel, the forests on the steep hillsides change from spruce to deciduous woodlands dominated by larch and birch. The previously clear water takes on a greater silt load, and gravel bars, through which the river braids, give way to sandbars in the lower reaches. The broader Peel River provides sufficient breadth and depth in certain locations for floatplane access. Most groups fly out from here. Some with more time will continue down the Peel to Fort McPherson. Here they rendezvous with the Dempster highway for the homeward journey.

Dall's Sheep—King of the Canyon Crags

In my mind the Dall's sheep which haunt the crags and spires of the northern river canyons seem akin to the majestic bald eagle. I admire them for their fleetness of foot and fearless mastery of steep rocky places. I appreciate them because they tend to frequent places where they may be easily spotted by river travelers passing below.

In his book *Mammals of the Canadian Rockies,* Dr. George Scotter explains that our wild sheep came to

LEFT: *Bonnet Plume Range, headwaters of the Snake River.*

OPPOSITE PAGE: *Unloading canoes at Duo Lakes, departure point for the Snake River.*

North America across the Bering land bridge which joined Alaska and Siberia. The sheep became isolated in different ice-free areas, or *refugia*. South of the river now known as the Columbia and the (U.S.) Snake River, the sheep evolved into bighorn sheep. In the Yukon and Alaska, they became thinhorn sheep. Dall's sheep are thinhorns. As the glaciers retreated the bighorns moved north into Alberta and British Columbia, but remained south of the range of the thinhorns.

Scotter comments that "mature thin horn rams are almost 150 cm (60 in.) in total length, about 94 cm (37 in.) in height at the shoulder, and weigh about 90 kg (200 lb.) . Females are somewhat smaller weighing about one-third less".

Perhaps the most impressive visual quality of the animal is the mature male's massive curled horns. Ochre in color, they can weigh up to 22 lbs (10 kg). They are attached to the skull with two separate layers of bone protecting the brain. "Ram's horns are weapons, shields, and indicators of rank," says Scotter. Horns are not shed, they remain for life. When a male is young, the circumfrencial rings that surround the horn are approximately an inch apart, but as the animal ages the distance between the new rings lessens. By the time the ram is five years old, his horns have grown to approximately two-thirds of their ultimate length and 90 percent of their basal circumference. The horns of the ewe are generally short and curved backwards.

Gregarious by nature, the sheep congregate in bands.

Scouting Second Canyon of the Snake River.

This allows them to draw upon "many eyes" for protection. The sheep's eyesight is believed to be the equivalent of humans aided by strong binoculars. Andy Russell, an outdoor writer who lives in the Rockies of Alberta, says of Dall's sheep: they may not be able to smell a dead horse or hear thunder but they can see through stone! Indeed, Dall's sheep seem to be able to detect minute movements at great distances. This trait, combined with the fact that they dwell in hard-to-reach terrain, serves as their main defensive strategy. During the summer season, the mature males sequester themselves from the females and young. The rams engage in much head-butting and posturing at this time to establish social hierarchy. The battle may last most of the day with the loser remaining in the band but in a position of subservience and without breeding privileges. Breeding takes place in the fall.

The lambs are born in May and soon engage in playful games. They scamper among the rocky heights, learning to use their well-adapted hooves. The unique footgear sports a concave, double-shelled hoof with a soft center that facilitates gripping rocks.

Perhaps my most poignant wildlife experience was on a fall day many years ago along the Nahanni River in Deadmen Valley. Ahead of us we spotted a wolf on the right side of the river. Captivated by the sighting, it took us a minute to realize that he was gazing longingly at a band of sheep on the opposite shore. So close and yet so far!

*Early morning mist on the
Snake.*

The Common Raven—*Corvus corax*— Bird's-Eye View of the River

Anyone who has watched the raven will know that it is anything but common. Named "Trickster" in some First Nations mythology, it is a smart bird capable of living up to this name.

In "Birds of the Canadian Rockies," Dr. Scotter

Historically, two First Nations groups frequented the Snake region. The Tetlit Gwich'in, from the Richardson Mountains in the north, came to the area to hunt caribou and fish for grayling, whitefish, and inconnu. With the establishment of the fur trade center of Fort McPherson in 1858, their patterns were altered as they shifted from community hunting and fishing to a more individual trapping and trading economy. From the south the Na-cho Ny'a'k Dun also followed the Bonnet Plume caribou herd into the Snake River drainage. They are descendents of the Northern Tuchone from the Stewart River area and often traded with the Gwich'in. Today their descendents live near the community of Mayo, which is approximately 220 miles (350 km) southeast of Duo Lakes.

These two groups crisscrossed the country via far-ranging trails used for hunting, gathering and trading. Most of the travel was overland, but stories tell of moose-skin boats used to carry families from winter hunting grounds to summer fishing camps. Today, both groups own land-claim settlements that reach into the Snake River corridor. These people once lived softly on the land and in harmony with the seasons. Modern settlements and the diminished fur industry has changed their traditional patterns. Today little evidence remains of their centuries of harvesting activities.

describes the raven as much larger than the American crow, with long pointed feathers on its throat which create a shaggy appearance, a rounded or wedge-shaped tail, and a heavier bill than the crow. The raven's ebony plumage has a metallic sheen on its under parts. This bird has a repertoire of at least 30 distinct calls which it uses to communicate with other ravens. The birds can also mimic the sounds of other animals, and even humans. You can sometimes be surprised by what Armstrong in *Guide to the Birds of Alaska* describes as a hoarse, croaking *kraaak*—almost a *quack*. The raven's other vocal variations include a hollow knocking sound and a melodious *kloo-klok*, which it often makes in flight.

Ravens nest on rock faces or conifers and do not migrate. They range from marine shores to mountain ridges and glaciers. These hardy birds are a common member of most northern communities and display incredible tenacity in the lowest sub-zero temperatures. They feed on seeds, berries, insects, and carrion. Opportunistic by nature, they will also eat anything an unwary traveler fails to protect (and don't think a cardboard box or plastic bag provides protection!). Of course the birds have a field day at garbage dumps. The raven is the consummate recycler.

A recent test measured the ingenuity of ravens compared with crows. A piece of meat was suspended on a string hanging from a perch. The attendant crows would dive at the meat and attempt to fly with it, resulting in obvious failure. The ravens would land on the perch and pull up the string with one foot. Raising the meat this way, it would step on the accumulated coils with the other foot, slowly retrieving the meat so that it could be eaten off the string on the perch. Northerners also tell of witnessing a group of ravens luring a dog away from its food dish allowing another of the tricksters to feast on the poor dog's kibble. Another testimony to the birds' wits is the way they learn to sit atop street lamps in the winter. By snuggling on top of the light sensor long enough, they can turn the light on in the middle of the day, generating a comfortable heat from the bulb.

The next time you watch a group of ravens talking to one another in the trees overhead, you can be assured they are talking about you. Perhaps it's a good thing we don't speak their language.

CHAPTER 6

Wind River (Yukon): A Lost Patrol

You will leave tomorrow morning for a patrol over the Fort McPherson trail, to locate the whereabouts of Inspector Fitzgerald's party. Indians from McPherson reported him on New Year's Day at Mountain Creek about 20 days to Dawson. I understand that at Hart River Divide no matter what route he took, he would have to cross this divide. I think it would be advisable to make for this point and take up his trail from there. I cannot give you any specific instructions; you will have to be guided by circumstances and your own judgment, bearing in mind that nothing is to stand in your way until you have got in touch with his party.

—ORDERS RECEIVED BY W.J. DEMPSTER OF THE ROYAL NORTH-WEST MOUNTED POLICE FROM SUPERINTENDENT A.E. SNYDER, IN COMMAND OF B DIVISION OF THE MOUNTIES, FEBRUARY 27, 1911.

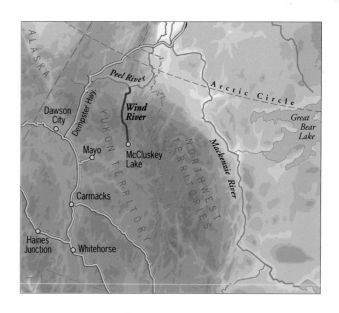

The Wind River is a beautiful and inviting watercourse for the canoeist who possesses some basic whitewater skills. To reach the river, paddlers usually take a day to drive from Whitehorse to the remote mining town of Mayo. At a floatplane base on the Stewart River, the canoes, food, gear and canoeists are loaded into a Single Otter aircraft. The ensuing flight is a dramatic introduction to the Wernecke Mountains. Peaks ranging from 5,000 to 6,000 feet (1650 to 1980 m), looming above the bush plane, make for a memorable highlight. Landing at McClusky Lake, the pilot drops off the group and bids good-bye. As the drone of the engine fades into the distance, the peaceful feel of wilderness emerges among the group. Some may call it silence, but it is anything but quiet. Breezes blowing in the willows and grasses, grayling jumping in the lake, and the happy jabber of companions fill the air with pleasant sounds. The mountain-ringed lake provides an opportunity to review canoe skills before embarking on the river. Tempting hiking routes and great fishing vie for any spare time.

A short portage trail links the lake to the river. The Wind is known for its crystal clear water. In these upper

Wind River whitewater. The Class II rapids provide excitement for those with whitewater canoeing skills.

reaches, the channel is narrow, gravely, shallow and braided. Canoeists floating on the current enjoy an uncommonly vivid view of the patina of boulders and pebbles that appear to slip by beneath the boat. The ragged Rackla Range dominates the skyline, and the gradient of the river is swift but not too intimidating for experienced canoeists.

The vicinity of Bond Creek offers a beautiful backdrop for camp and a hike into the alpine that is rewarded with panoramic vistas. The sights, sounds and smells of camp on the river are delightful. While dry driftwood crackles in the firebox, the guides create baked delicacies in cast aluminum Dutch ovens. Campers can be seen lazing in the sun reading books,

ABOVE: *The morning ritual of loading canoes on a sunny morning in the Central Yukon.*

OPPOSITE PAGE: *Wind River Camp.*

Origin: Werneke Range of the
Mackenzie Mountains
Length: 190 miles (280 km)
Drop: 2400 feet (800 m)
Completion: confluence with
the Peel River
Status: unprotected

Perhaps even more fascinating is the prehistoric history of the region, 22,000 to 30,000 years ago after the recession of the Selwyn lobe of the Wisconsin ice sheet of the Pleistocene Glaciation. At this time, much of the planet's water was frozen in glaciers and the oceans were shallower. Because of this, the region between Siberia and Alaska, now known as the Bering Strait, was dry. In this barren condition, species were able to migrate from Asia into North America across a land bridge. This likely included our own kind, but some of the others were more exotic. The Wooly Mammoth, related to the elephant, was but one species. Giant beaver (standing chest high to a man), ferocious scimitar cats, sheep and muskoxen were all residents. It is thought that other species such as caribou actually evolved in Buringia. By definition this area stretched from the Kolyma River in Siberia to the Mackenzie River in Canada, a distance of 2,000 miles (3200 km). The notion of the land bridge was first hypothesized by the Swedish botanist Eric Hultén, who proposed the former existence of a land bridge where Bering Strait exists today. Vitus Jonassen Bering was a Danish explorer who served as an officer in the Russian navy. In 1725, Peter the Great appointed Bering to explore the coast of Siberia. By sailing through the strait, Bering proved for the first time that Asia and North America were not joined. The strait, Bering Sea, the land bridge, and Bering Island were named after him.

Humans likely arrived prior to 14,000 years ago, having gradually moved through Asia from Africa. This is a remarkable evolution of adaptation and technology when one considers the circumstances involved. As our ancestors moved northward, they learned how to live in the Far

casting a fishing line into an eddy or roaming the vicinity with binoculars seeking the next bird sighting. In July the sun sets well after midnight and it is easy to loose track of time and end up in bed much later than one's habitual time.

Back on the river, the scenery continues to unfold in diverse tableaus. Bear River contributes to the flow where it meets the Wind. The name reminds everyone to be watchful for a sighting of the elusive grizzly. Royal Mountain appears on the horizon with regal splendor. On its eastern shore the Wind courses beneath steep mountain slopes. Farther downstream, at the confluence with the Little Wind River, it squeezes out of the confines of the Illtyd Range into a broader, sprawling valley.

North. With artifacts made by hand from stone, bone, sinew, wood, fiber, and moss, they tailored skin clothing and designed secure dwellings. Employing the use of alternative fuels such as animal dung, finely broken bone, and fat or oil in areas lacking woody plants, they developed expert control of fire. They learned to travel over rugged terrain of snow and ice, and it is likely that they also invented watercraft with which to cross dangerously cold rivers. Another easily overlooked achievement was how they learned to cope with long hours of winter darkness. To develop these skills would have required a profound knowledge of biology, including the nutritional and medicinal properties of many plants and the habits and anatomy of many animals. These people became experts at finding geological deposits that contained stone suitable for flaking into tools and grinding into pigments. The use of oral tradition to pass along the knowledge gained would have required that they were great storytellers who entertained and educated themselves by passing on oral histories and knowledge from one generation to another.

There is no question that the remains of creatures from these ancient times are buried and preserved in permafrost under our Wind River campsites. As one paddles down the Wind today, marveling at the stunning scenery, it is profoundly moving to reflect on these long ago people and the knowledge and wisdom that sustained them in this land when it was surrounded by ice. The thought of crossing or traveling the river in a skin boat is beyond comprehension for modern travelers. If you are up early enough in the morning and peer quietly through the mist, you may be lucky enough to catch a glimpse of a large form as it lumbers through the willows. What else could it be but a wooly mammoth?

At Hungry Creek, the landscape is dominated by Mount Deception. One can't help but wonder what stories loom behind these names. In truth, the pleasures enjoyed by modern river travelers on the Wind were not shared by some past visitors to this valley.

A hundred years ago, at the time of the great Klondike Gold Rush, the southern travelers who found themselves wintering on the Wind were not enthused. A small band of stampeders were forced to spend the winter at a rough camp, which they named Wind City. It was home to between 50 and 80 people during the winter of 1898-99. Following the grueling winter those people continued upstream on the Wind, over the pass to the Stewart River and then downstream to Dawson City.

Many groups have searched for the remaining artifacts of Wind City, but it seems that it has been washed away by the shifting channels and spring floods of the river.

As the river approaches the Peel River, the valley bottom continues to broaden and is heavily forested. It was in this region that another famous group traveled the river, but in the dark of winter. In December of 1910, Inspector Francis J. Fitzgerald of the North-West Mounted Police and his fabled "Lost Patrol" began their journey by dogsled, far away on Herschel Island, at the mouth of the Firth River. For some reason they neglected to engage a native guide for the remaining 475 mile (760 km) leg, when they passed through the post of Fort McPherson. This was to lead to their peril. In the dark of the month of January, they floundered in the Wind River Valley, making vain attempts on the wrong tributaries to cross over into the Stewart River drainage. Finally, nearing the end of their supplies and realizing their error, they turned back. Weather and trail conditions conspired against them. Temperatures dropped to -65 F below zero and the group finally perished only 70 miles (112 km) short of Fort McPherson. Their grim fate was discovered by a rescue party, led by Corporal W. J. D. Dempster from Dawson City. The men of the patrol are buried in Fort McPherson on the Peel River, and Dempster was honored with having Canada's most northerly highway named after him.

Thankfully, canoeists benefit from the summer reality that the river flows downhill. The opportunities for becoming lost are few and the chances of a fate like the lost patrol are remote. As long as one can navigate the many braids of the Wind's channels, the Peel River inevitably looms ahead. Once on the Peel, the current courses past the junction with the Bonnet Plume and Snake Rivers. After negotiating a short canyon, paddlers pull ashore on a gravely shoal named Taco Bar. Here the river is deep enough to safely accommodate the floats of the Otter landing on the river. Another spectacular flight delivers the travelers back to Mayo with a cargo of fond memories.

Why Do Rivers Meander?

The tortuous, flat turns of a meandering river often cause paddlers to travel nearly twice the distance the crow flies to the same destination. Many times while on the water I have asked myself what causes the river to twist in the first place? Virtually every river meanders, some more dramatically than others. Why would the water not follow a straight line as it accommodates the law of gravity? Why does the river not straighten after negotiating an obstacle?

The fact that rivers meander is relatively common knowledge among those who travel along them. Obviously, the erosion caused by flowing water is the mechanism; centrifugal force creates faster water on the outside of a bend. The faster water on the outside erodes the outer bank and the resulting silt is deposited in the slower water of an inside bend farther

Moose feeding on aquatic plants.

downstream, thereby accentuating the meander. But this does not explain why a river meanders in a persistent looping pattern.

My curiosity about this phenomenon was satiated with an article I found in the July / August 1993 issue of Canadian Geographic. From it I learned that there are many forces that will disturb the theoretical perfect flow of a stream of water. David M. Baird and Dane Lanken explain that fluids in motion have an inherent instability, and that a river's inevitable looping meanders are due to the column of water vibrating like a rigid body. Ted Hickin, an earth scientist at Simon Fraser University, explains that it is much like the "wind sheering down a flag and how the flag flaps in folds." Fluid sheering down a channel behaves similarly. Eventually one wave length dominates and turns up in the shape of the river.

A literal spin-off of meandering is the Oxbow Lake. As the ever-expanding loop of the meander reaches approximately 2.5 times the river's width, it stops growing. The river often "bites off" the loop, taking a shortcut across the neck of the meander. Flying in to the Nahanni, you may witness many of these meanders, dried up, in the Liard flood plain. These former meanders are known as a meander scar.

Hicken goes on to state that the rate at which meanders form and reform depends on many factors—the amount of sediment a river carries, its current, and type of material in it banks.

Twin Otter without floats touches down on a remote landing strip.

With this answered, I have one less question to ask myself as I paddle the tortuous flat meanders.

The DHC-6 Twin Otter—A Flying Machine that's Synonymous with Northern Rivers

Questions about the equipment we use are frequently asked prior to a trip. It is surprising how seldom anyone inquires about the aircraft which will carry us away from civilization to the "middle of nowhere." The good news is that we employ the best available planes to suit the task. We can select Cessnas, Beavers, Single Otters, or the ubiquitous Twin Otter, depending on the destination. What's most interesting about the aircraft is their history and the unique performance characteristics that set them apart from any other. Before take-off, group members can be seen loading gear from a wooden dock into a floating aircraft. A colorful pilot, clad in jeans and a plaid shirt, taxis nonchalantly for take-off—in a high performance plane that costs more per mile to operate than a Learjet! The efficiency of the aircraft further masks the marvel. As the plane soars among the mountain peaks, the passengers photograph the stunning scenery below while the turboprop engines hum reliably. Everyone relaxes with confidence as the pilot smoothly lands the aircraft in a remarkably short distance on the water and unloads the payload of two weeks' worth of food, gear, and canoes or rafts. Indeed, more than a few guests have commented upon landing:

"If the trip was over now, I would have gotten more than my money's worth already!"

The story and record of the Twin Otter is impressive. It followed in the footsteps of the De Havilland Beaver and Single Otter. First manufactured in 1965, there were eventually 844 Twin Otters flying throughout the world. The last one flew out of the factory and into service in 1988, and the fleet remains in high demand around the world. Anywhere that short take-off and landing (STOL) characteristics are required, the Twin Otter shines.

The Twin Otter is able to land in nearly the distance required for a helicopter, and it does so with far greater efficiency and economy.

The secret of the Otter's STOL abilities lies in two key areas. Its wings are designed for maximum lift at low

RIGHT: *Arctic poppy.*

OPPOSITE PAGE: *Red fox in flowers.*

speeds. They achieve this via the shape and a design that discourages air from "spilling off" the wingtips, thereby enhancing lift. The other amazing quality is the ability to actually reverse the thrust of the propellers powered by the Pratt and Whitney turbojet engine. While the propellers turn at high speeds, the angle of the propeller blades can be changed so that the thrust is completely reversed. The effect of this quality is impressive. When the plane lands on a small lake or gravel bar, the reverse thrust is akin to applying the brakes in a car. Without it the pilot would require a far greater distance to land, which would eliminate many short landing strips that are actually made viable due to the Twin Otter's superior performance. The plane's versatility is enhanced by the fact that it can be outfitted with floats, skis, or over inflated "tundra tires" allowing it to operate in any

season. The Twin Otter is the favorite of armed forces for search and rescue missions, which is why you will often see it on the television news in dramatic acts of rescue. From the upper reaches of the Amazon River to the Arctic and Antarctic, the DHC-6s are legendary in service. The Royal Canadian Mounted Police maintain a fleet of DHC-6s to support northern outposts. Here the planes are used for everything from rescue to surveillance missions. They are also occasionally loaded with furniture and family goods when an RCMP officer is transferred to a distant outpost.

Jacques Harvey is one of the dedicated pilots who specializes in flying the Twin Otters. Through his company, South Nahanni Airways, he expertly manages our flights into the Nahanni region. With more than 5,000 hours of flying time in the DHC-6, Jacques is a true master and continues to mentor a generation of co-pilots in the peaks of the Ragged Range.

Nothing is casual about the operation of the aircraft. Each flight is a carefully calculated mission which requires precise attention to a multitude of details from air temperature to payload.

The resulting performance allows us to reach remote wilderness areas safely and consistently and to focus our attention on enjoying the trip of a lifetime.

ABOVE: *Wandering Tattler.*

OPPOSITE PAGE: *Midnight flight past a rain storm on the Wind River.*

CHAPTER 7

Stikine River (British Columbia/Alaska): Spatsizi Plateau Wilderness Provincial Park to the Inside Passage of Alaska

The Stickeen [sic] was, perhaps, the best known of the rivers that cross the Coast Range, because it was the best way to the Mackenzie River Cassiar gold-mines. It is about three hundred and fifty miles long, and is navigable for small steamers, a hundred and fifty miles to Glenora, and sometimes to Telegraph Creek, fifteen miles further. It first pursues a westerly course through grassy plains darkened here and there with groves of spruce and pine; then, curving southward and receiving numerous tributaries from the north, it enters the Coast Range and sweeps it through a magnificent canon three thousand to five thousand feet deep, and more than a hundred miles long. The majestic cliffs and mountains forming the cañon walls display endless variety of form and sculpture, and are wonderfully adorned and enlivened with glaciers and waterfalls, while throughout almost its whole extent the floor is a flowery landscape garden, like Yosemite. The most striking features are the glaciers, hanging over the cliffs, descending the side cañons and pushing forward to the river, greatly enhancing the wild beauty of all the others.
—JOHN MUIR, TRAVELING UP THE STIKINE FROM ITS MOUTH IN 1879.
FROM *TRAVELS IN ALASKA*, BY JOHN MUIR, PUBLISHED IN 1915

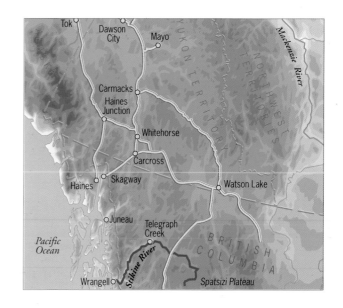

The coastal Tlingit people called it "Stikine," the great river. Although the Stikine lies south of the 60th parallel and is (theoretically) accessible by road, it represents one of the most diverse and dramatic "canoeable" rivers on the West Coast of the continent.

Issuing forth from the glaciers of the Spatsizi Plateau, the meltwater, which will become the Stikine, pools in the crystalline waters of Tuaton Lake. It is in these upper

Midnight sunset colors over the Inside Passage of Southeast Alaska, near Wrangell.

Origin: Tuaton Lake, Spatsizi Plateau, British Columbia

Length: 313 miles (500 km)

Drop: 3,825 feet (1200 m)

Completion: Stikine estuary Gulf of Alaska

Unique Status: Stikine originates in Spatsizi Provincial Park, leaves the park before the Grand Canyon of the Stikine and crosses the Canadian–U.S. border into Tongass National Forest.

RIGHT: *Adoogacho Falls, a short hike from the upper Stikine.*

OPPOSITE PAGE: *Whitewater of the upper Stikine.*

reaches of the massive 19,227 square miles (49,800 sq. km) watershed that the Stikine subtly begins its course.

As the birthplace of the Stikine, the Spatsizi Plateau has much to recommend it. It is a pristine wilderness treasure. Nestled behind the Coast Mountains to the west, the region is in a precipitation shadow. The shallow snowpack of the winter provides ideal alpine wintering grounds for many species. The Osborne mountain caribou herd of approximately 3,000 animals shares the range with Dall's sheep and mountain goats.

At 4970 ft (1,600 m), the plateau is a spectacular alpine region that includes the stark cinder cones of the Mount Edziza volcanoes. These little-known volcanoes were active 10,000 years ago. Few Canadians realize that the northwest corner of British Columbia is dominated by volcanic peaks and ancient lava beds!

The Stikine departs the lake as a small stream and descends a broad, glacial-carved valley. Here lively rapids are interspersed with long stretches of flat swift water. The extensive forests of the valley bottom are home to moose, grizzly, and black bears. The river cuts through the center of the forested valley, a long way from the overlooking alpine slopes. In these upper reaches, the vegetation remains that of the boreal forest; the thick growth of the coastal rain forest waits below.

Nearly 60 feeding tributaries ensure that the Stikine swells in size and speed as it reaches the edge of the plateau. In an abrupt gash in the land, the river drops 930 feet (300 m) into the maw of a narrow chasm—the

Grand Canyon of the Stikine. For the middle one-third of its journey, the river is a tumultuous cataract that defies navigation. Negotiated by only a handful of paddlers to date, this part of the Stikine was slated to be dammed for electrical power in the 1980s. Fortunately, however, this did not happen. Today it is home to 300 to 400 mountain goats. These goats, whose white coats take on a red color from the iron oxide dust in the rock, are the namesake of the region. Spatsizi is a Tahltan word that means "land of the red goat."

Before leaving this cleft in the earth's crust, some of it so narrow that it never receives direct sunlight—the course of the Stikine is directed by a 10,000-year-old lava flow. The volcanic rock is the product of the last eruption of Mt. Edziza.

Within a few miles of the lower breech of the canyon, the river smooths and despite its vast volume and speed takes on a surprising peacefulness. The confluence with the Tahltan River is a traditional fishing ground of the Tahltan people and a site of trading with the coastal Tlingit. For centuries the river has provided a route for these two cultures to trade goods, which have included eulachon oil, herring eggs, dried salmon, copper, and furs, as well as articles obtained from Russian traders on the coast.

Not far downstream lies the picturesque gold-rush town of Telegraph Creek. The village is now accessible by a precarious road but formerly could only be reached by river steamer from the coast. At times in its history it has served as a Hudson's Bay post, a mission, a jumping-off place for more than 10,000 gold-rush stampeders and as a Tahltan First Nations community. The "lower level" of town, along the riverbank, is relegated to the church and commerce, while the Tahltan village is spread out on the plateau above.

Looking to the west from Telegraph Creek, one sees the telltale white snowcaps of the coastal mountain to the west, foreshadowing the massive sprawling glaciers ahead.

Here the cottonwoods and fir of the valley bottom seem to swell in diameter with each passing mile. The understory vegetation becomes lush and begins to include flora found in moist climes. The beautiful peaks on either side of the river are alluring but the thick vegetation, complete with spiny devil's club, repels the hiker except at strategic trails.

As the vegetation thickens to rain-forest lushness, the valley glaciers grow in number and size. These majestic ice sheets crawl toward the river. The tributary valleys are rugged and active, with glacial activity sometimes blocking off stream flow and creating lakes. This can lead to a *Jokulhlaup*, an Icelandic term for a glacial lake outburst which temporarily floods the valley. The main channel of the Stikine is littered with trunks of massive trees, eroded from the riverbanks. These pile up in the countless logjams that seem to mark every bend in the river. While posing a very real hazard to river travelers, the strainer effect of the logjams serves to

Sarah McGregar greets visitors to the Stikine Riversong Café and General Store in the remote Gold Rush town of Telegraph Creek.

~~~~~~

~~~~~~

RIVERS AS GREEN CORRIDORS

To see the "big picture" of the relationships between rivers and the land, we must exchange detailed topographic map for one with a larger view. Certain relationships then become more apparent. In the case of the coastal mountain rivers such as the Stikine, Alsek, and Tatshenshini, it is the link they forge between the interior and the coast. This is an important dynamic. In the mountainous northern interior of British Columbia, Yukon and Alaska, there are a number of riverine jewels that form significant watersheds flowing west from the interior through the Coast Mountains and out to the ocean. Obviously not a difficult geographic idea to grasp. What has intrigued me are the circumstances that these rivers create as they plunge toward the coast.

The phenomenon of the green corridor and its beauty was not lost on John Muir. When he traveled the Alaska coast in 1879, he reported:

"The most interesting of the short excursions we made from Fort Wrangell was the one up the Stickeen [sic] River to the head of steam navigation. From Mt. St. Elias the coast range extends in a broad lofty chain beyond the southern boundary of the territory, gashed by stupendous cañons, each of which carries a lively river, though most of them are comparatively short, as their highest sources lie in the icy solitudes of the

create eddies downstream, which aid the upstream travel of the spawning salmon, headed for the tributaries of their birth.

Downriver, a chilled stream, tumbling through a rocky bed, provides a signal to travelers that they have arrived in the vicinity of Great Glacier Lake. A short hike through the lush overhanging moss of the cathedral-like forest brings one to the breathtaking beautiful lake. It was formed when the Great Glacier carved a massive basin, which filled with water as the glacier receded. Those who portage their canoe the short distance across the old terminal moraine to the lake will be rewarded by the opportunity to paddle among the massive icebergs calved from the face of the Great Glacier. The sight of these icebergs becomes all the more awe-inspiring when one learns that only one-tenth of each berg is visible above the water!

Below the lake, the river flows toward the boundary of Alaska. It emerges from the Coast Mountains and crosses the Alaska Panhandle to empty into the Pacific Ocean. First it passes the confluence with its largest tributary, the Iskut River. A commercial salmon fishery *range within forty or fifty miles of the coast. A few, however, of these foaming, roaring streams— the Alsek, Chilkat, Chilkoot, Taku, Stickeen, and perhaps others—head beyond the range with some of the southwest branches of the Mackenzie and Yukon."*

Most of these rivers slice through vastly glaciated and mountainous terrain. The chief effect is a corridor and eco-region through which species may move between the coast and the interior. The maintenance of a passage by these river valleys creates rich ecosystems through which life surges.

The remoteness of these corridors promotes the richness and productivity of the ecosystems and,

of course, enhances the attractiveness for people like us who wish to escape into the wilderness.

Diversity is the key, with change around every bend in the river. The transition from the dry interior climate into the moist coastal air brings changes in ecosystems—most evident in dramatic plant changes. The passage from alpine forest to rain forest is as extreme as it can get!

The tall mountain spires which catch moisture at high altitudes enhance the contrast, along with huge sprawling glaciers, which create their own climate; some actually "calve" bergs into the rivers and lakes. The resulting drama is truly captivating.

exists here on the Stikine. Like most, it is in a troubled state with numbers dwindling.

An ancient and abandoned customs house stands at the U.S.–Canada border. It serves as a reminder of the riverboat traffic that plied these waters at a time when the Stikine was truly viewed as a highway into the northern interior of the continent. It seems a ludicrous monument in a day and age when no more than a handful of people descends the river each year.

Tongass National Forest begins at the American border. Not far downstream, the savvy paddler can follow a series of channels that yield a sweet reward—Chief Shakes Hotsprings. The U.S. Forest Service has modestly developed these natural sources of hot water with a boardwalk and cedar hot tubs. On a clear day, the view from the springs is stunning.

Downstream the river begins to widen around islands that guard the Stikine estuary. Millennia of deposition of river sediments have created a fertile oasis. Here, the Pacific Coast's migratory flyway finds a focal point. The rich biotic conditions also provide a fertile environment for countless species of fish and shellfish.

On an island out in the delta of the Stikine lies the small town of Wrangell, Alaska, formerly the site of a Tlingit village. It was first settled by Russian traders in 1834 and called Fort Dionysius. The name was changed to Fort Stikine in 1840 when the Alaska Panhandle was leased to the Hudson's Bay Company. When the Panhandle was sold to the United States in 1867, the name was finally changed to Fort Wrangell. Both a fishing and logging community and a small port, the community is charting its way through the challenges of the 21st century. River travelers receive a warm welcome, but it doesn't take much to rouse a stirring debate among locals about the future as it relates to resource-based economies and the security of the community. Hopefully they will find a way to continue living in harmony with the Stikine—the great river.

Beaver (*Castor Canadensis*): River Engineer

Beavers are found within virtually all of the treed bounds of our country. We are likely to encounter them on all of our river expeditions except for ones in the treeless tundra. Known for industrious lodge and dam-building, these aquatic rodents are heavyweights, coming in at 35 to 65 pounds (16 to 30 kgs) as adults.

In *Mammals of the Canadian Rockies* Dr. Scotter reports that the hind and front feet are different in both structure and function. Broad hind feet with five long webbed toes propel the beaver through the water and support it on soft muddy ground. Each hind foot has split and serrated claws that are movable and come together like pliers, serving as a comb for grooming.

The beaver's front feet, which are not webbed, are

RIGHT: *Red Fox in silver phase.*

OPPOSITE PAGE:
Canoeing the upper Stikine in the Spatsizi Plateau.

RIGHT: *Alpine slopes above Tuaton Lake, the headwaters of the Stikine.*

OPPOSITE PAGE: *Canoeing among the icebergs on Great Glacier Lake. The bergs weigh many tons and "calve" off the Great Glacier with a booming, explosive impact. As they float serenely on the surface, they can split and roll with tremendous effect. It's impossible to predict when this will happen, so paddlers are advised to keep at a safe distance.*

Old-growth rain forest on the terminal moraine that separates Great Glacier Lake from the Stikine River. The trail to the lake leads through this lush forest.

small and dexterous, with long sharp claws suitable for digging and carrying a variety of materials such as sticks, stones, and mud for construction of dams. Secretions from anal glands, applied to the fur with the hind and front feet, provide waterproofing.

Large incisor teeth dominate the beaver's face. They make quick work of severing aspens, poplars and willows which provide both food and lodge-and-dam building materials. The ingenious dams are built and maintained to create ponds deep enough to avoid freezing to the bottom in winter. Lodges are constructed in the ponds with underwater entrances and a sleeping chamber that lies above the surface level. The industrious animals store green branches underwater for use during the winter. Both the nostrils and ears are equipped with valves that can be closed for underwater swimming. The oversized lungs allow for up to 15 minutes of submersion.

Perhaps the animal's most unique feature is its flat, muscular scaled tail. You may have heard the "gunshot" slap on the water of a beaver tail, used to alert other beavers of danger as it dives. The beaver also uses its tail as a rudder while swimming and to counterbalance weight when carrying heavy branches in the front paws. The tail is also an important energy storage vault. By winter, the mass of the beaver tale will double in stored fat. But by spring it will shrink by 50%. The First Nations people considered the fatty tail a delicacy. This is easy to understand when one considers that much of the wild meat they consumed was very lean.

Creating dams that flood ponds is only one way in which the beaver dramatically shapes our landscape. As the flooded pond eutrophies and fills in after the beavers have taken all they can of the surrounding trees, a new meadow emerges from the old pond. Many alpine valleys have flat meadow areas that began as flooded beaver ponds.

Perhaps no animal has played such a pivotal role in the shaping of a nation and its rivers. After all, it was the hair of this noble rodent that drove the fur trade, which, in turn, fueled the exploration of Canada by Europeans. The desire for social recognition as exemplified by a beaver felt chapeau, was the driving force behind many tales of glory, heroism, tragedy and even (perhaps mostly) buffoonery.

For most of a century, the image of the beaver has dominated as the logo of Parks Canada. Of course, insiders are amused that a rodent was chosen to represent the august organization. But in truth, a more fitting candidate could not be found!

CHAPTER 8

Burnside River (Nunavut Territory): Arctic Wonderland—Caribou and Cotton Grass

The Burnside River is a classic tundra waterway flowing into the Arctic Ocean. Originating at Contwoyto Lake, it flows across the Contwoyto Plateau, which rises out of the Precambrian Shield. This plateau has an average elevation of 1,500 feet (460 m) and is characterized by granite boulder till mixed with sand. Eskers, gravely teardrop-shaped hills formed under ancient glaciers, are common features on this rolling landscape. The hills above the river valley provide impressive views of the surrounding countryside, with small crystal-clear lakes dotting the terrain. Isolated and rugged, the river offers exciting whitewater rafting and canoeing, dramatic scenery and abundant wildlife. The views are dramatic with undulating tundra punctuated by narrow canyons, waterfalls, and sandy beaches. As it nears the ocean, the Burnside enters the Wilberforce Hills region, characterized by deep river valleys, spectacular cliffs, and canyons. This is especially evident along the final few miles of the river. Here there are many birds of prey. Notably, peregrines and gyrfalcons, as well as golden eagles and rough-legged hawks. These magnificent birds make their nests on the rocky cliffs along the river.

Good hiking opportunities are frequent along the entire course of the river and wildlife is plentiful. The freezing and thawing of the sod above the underlying permafrost yields an undulating surface of tussocks. Hikers often bring along a pair of walking sticks. These help to keep their balance on this uneven surface. Caribou, muskoxen, wolves, and the occasional grizzly bear are the dominant large mammals. Wolverines, foxes, arctic hares, arctic ground squirrels, and several other small mammals are also found. Anyone predisposed to fishing can enjoy arctic char, lake trout, arctic grayling, and whitefish, which inhabit both the river and the attached lakes.

The caribou of the Bathurst herd usually cross the

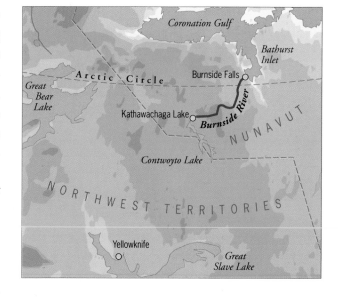

Burnside River campsite. The broad expanse of treeless tundra provides panoramic views. With no trees to obstruct sightings, wildlife viewing is exceptional in this environment.

Origin: Contwoyto Lake, Nunavut

Length: 161 miles (258 km) 128 miles (205 km) from Kathawachaga Lake to Bathurst Inlet

Drop: 1275 feet (420m)

Completion: Bathurst Inlet on the Arctic Ocean

Unique Status: unprotected

An arctic wolf faces the camera.

September 14, 1820—This morning the officers being assembled round a small fire, Perrault presented each of us with a small piece of meat which he had saved from his own allowance. It was received with great thankfulness, and such an act of self-denial and kindness being totally unexpected in a Canadian voyageur filled our eyes with tears. In directing our course to a river issuing from the lake [Contwoyto Lake], we met Credit, who communicated the joyful intelligence of his having killed two deer [caribou] in the morning. We instantly halted, and having shared the deer that was nearest to us, prepared breakfast. After which the other deer was sent for, and we went down to the [Burnside] river, which was about three hundred yards wide, and flowed through a broken rocky channel. Having searched for a part where the current was most smooth, the canoe was placed in the water at the head of a rapid, and St. Germain, Solomon, Belanger and I, embarked in order to cross. We went from the shore very well, but in mid-channel the canoe became difficult to manage under our burden as the breeze was fresh. The current drove us to the edge of the rapid, when Belanger unluckily applied his paddle to avert the apparent danger of being forced down it, and lost his balance. The canoe was overset in consequence in the middle of the rapid. We fortunately kept hold of it, until we touched a rock where the water did not reach higher than our waists; here we kept our footing, notwithstanding the strength of the current, until the water was emptied out of the canoe. Belanger then held the canoe steady whilst St. Germain placed me in it, and afterwards embarked himself in a very dexterous manner. It was impossible however to embark Belanger, as the canoe would have been hurried down the rapid the moment he should have raised his foot from the rock on which he stood. We were, therefore, compelled to leave him in his perilous situation. We had not gone twenty yards before the canoe, striking on a sunken rock, went down. The place being shallow, we were again enabled to empty it, and the third attempt brought us to the shore. In the mean time Belanger was suffering extremely, immersed to his middle in the center of a rapid, the temperature of which was very little above the freezing point, and the upper part of his body covered with wet clothes, exposed in a temperature not much above zero, to a strong breeze. He called piteously for relief, and St. Germain on his return endeavored to embark him, but in vain. The canoe was hurried down the rapid, and when he landed he was

rendered by the cold incapable of further exertion, and Adam attempted to embark Belanger but found it impossible. An attempt was next made to carry out to him a line, made of the slings of the men's loads. This also failed, the current acting so strongly upon it, as to prevent the canoe from steering, and it was finally broken and carried away downstream. At length, when Belanger's strength seemed almost exhausted, the canoe reached him with a small cord belonging to one of the nets, and he was dragged perfectly senseless through the rapid. By the direction of Dr. Richardson, he was instantly stripped, and being rolled up in blankets, two men undressed themselves and went to bed with him: but it was some hours before he recovered his warmth and sensations. As soon as Belanger was placed in his bed, the officers sent over my blankets, and a person made a fire. Augustus brought the canoe over, and in returning was obliged to descend both rapids, before he could get across the stream; which hazardous service he performed with the greatest coolness and judgement. It is impossible to describe my sensations as I witnessed the various unsuccessful attempts to relieve Belanger. The distance prevented my seeing distinctly what was going on, and I continued pacing up and down

the rock on which I landed, regardless of the coldness of my drenched and stiffened garments. The canoe, in every attempt to reach him was hurried down the rapid, and was lost to view amongst the rocky islets, with a rapidity that seemed to threaten certain destruction; once, indeed, I fancied that I saw it overwhelmed with waves. Such an event would have been fatal to the whole party. Separated as I was from my companions, without gun, ammunition, hatchet, or the means of making a fire, and in wet clothes, my doom would have been sealed. My companions, too, driven to the necessity of coasting the lake, must have sunk under the fatigue of having to round its innumerable arms and bays, which, as we have learned from the Indians, are very extensive. By the goodness of Providence, however, we were spared at that time, and some of us have been permitted to offer up our thanksgivings, in a civilized land, for the signal deliverances we then afterwards experienced.

By this accident I had the misfortune to loose my portfolio, containing my journal from Fort Enterprise, together with all the astronomical and meteorological observations made during the descent of the Copper-Mine River, and along the sea-coast. I was in the habit of carrying it

Discovering a Peregrine falcon is a chance occurrence.

~~~~~~

~~~~~~~~~~~~~~~~~~~~~~~~

strapped across my shoulders, but had taken it off on entering the canoe, to reduce the upper weight. The results of most of the observations for latitude and longitude had been registered in the sketch-books, so that we preserved the requisites for the construction of the chart. The meteorological observations, not having being copied, were lost. My companions, Dr. Richardson, Mr. Back, and Mr. Hood, had been so careful in noting every occurrence in their journals, that the loss of mine would fortunately be well supplied. These friends immediately offered me their documents, and every assistance in drawing up another narrative, of which kindness I availed myself at the earliest opportunity afterwards.
—FROM THE JOURNAL OF SIR JOHN FRANKLIN'S JOURNEY TO THE POLAR SEA IN THE YEARS 1819-20-21-22. THE FIRST EUROPEAN TRAVELERS ON THE BURNSIDE RIVER—DESCRIBING A VERY BAD DAY—BUT NOT THE WORST.

Thousands of jewel-like lakes dot the tundra. A short hike from the river can reveal a lake that may not have seen human visitation in decades or longer.

Burnside River in the latter part of June, also the season for an explosion of color across the tundra. Every square mile of the land seems awash with a rainbow of wildflowers—a stark contrast to the barren vastness of the landscape. *"Barrenland beauties"* is how as botanist and author Page Burt refers to the stunning array of flowers. They blossom quickly to take advantage of the twenty-four hours of light in the short northern growing season. These delicate-looking specimens have adapted to survive this austere environment. Some have parabola-shaped petals which focus heat from the sun's rays. Others have tiny hairs that harbor just enough warm air to make a difference. All of the plants keep close to the ground, an essential strategy in a treeless land where the air is seldom calm. Several varieties of lichen and moss also carpet the ground. The net result is a land that is anything but barren.

The Burnside area has been well used by the Inuit for generations. The numerous archeological sites along the river mark their lifetimes and passage through the area. Rings of rocks were used each season to anchor the edges of skin tents. Gravesites of piled rocks can be seen at several locations. Kayak racks made of pairs of stones forming a "V" notch can be found in old camps. These would have supported and protected the skin boat from the ground and rodents.

The most important known site is on the tiny island of Nadlok, located just downstream from Kathawachaga Lake. The name in Inuktituk means "place where the deer cross." It is no coincidence that river travelers often spot caribou in this area. On this island in the summers of 1985 and 1986, the National Museum of Civilization unearthed more than 40,000 segments of caribou antlers that were thought to have formed the framework

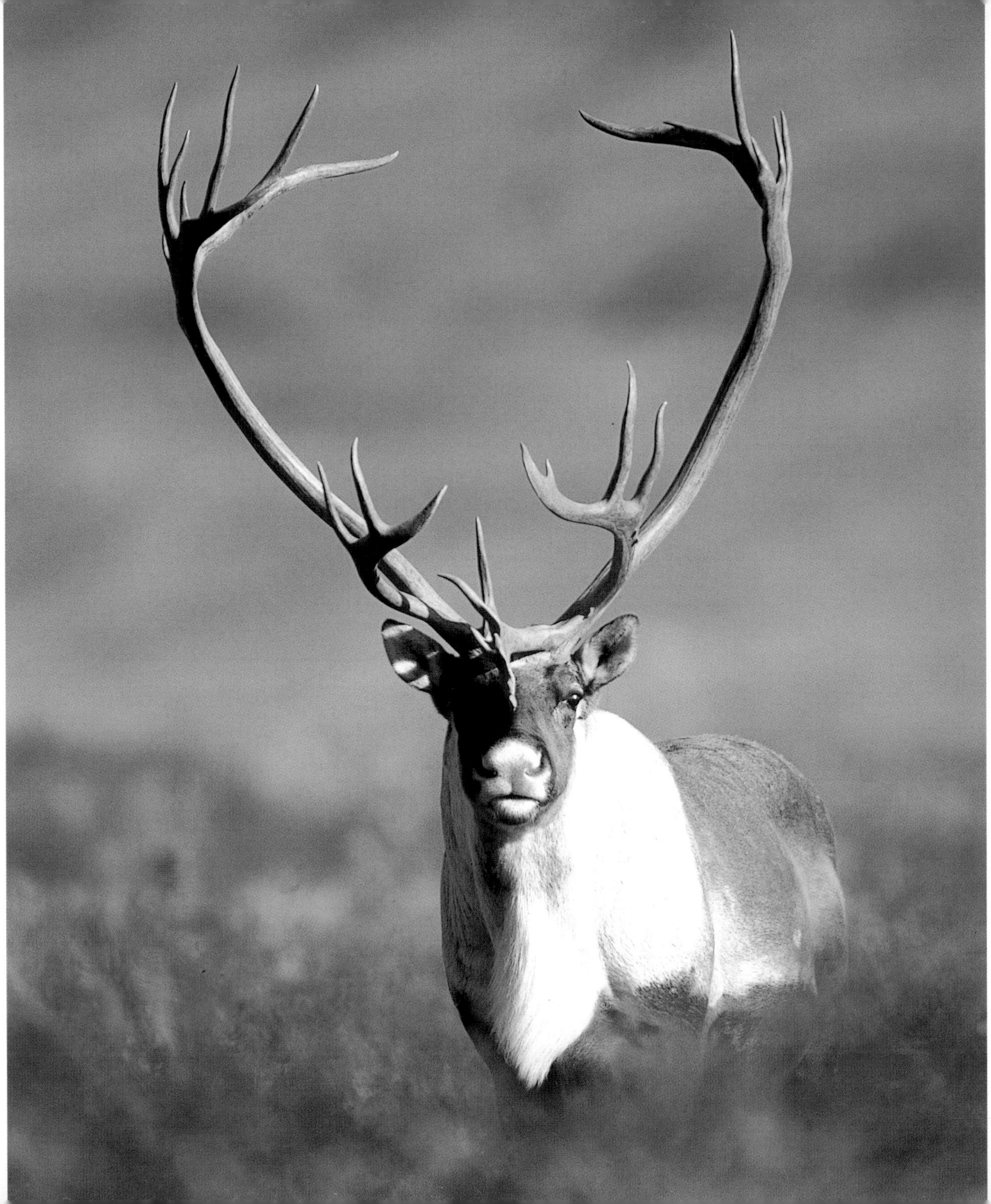

At the top of the list of Burnside River highlights is the Bathurst caribou herd. Over the ridges they stream, a seemingly endless cavalcade of hooves, click-clacking on the ends of gangly legs. Cows and two-week-old calves making their way south from the rocky calving grounds on the coast east of Bathurst Inlet around the Ellice River. On this springtime pilgrimage that crosses the Burnside River these curious creatures sometimes clog the river, swimming in front of your raft. They leave a noticeable trail of hollow, buoyant hair which lines the shore for miles downstream of their crossing. Camp amid the caribou migration is a magical vortex. Comprising a herd of 300,000, they walk through camp, spooking at human movement and then coming closer to investigate the source. Only recently born, the calves can out-run the lingering and patient wolves. Overhead a circling golden eagle watches for hours, looking for a suitable candidate. A few hours before, this rolling tundra would have seemed vacant of all but plant life. Now it teems with snorting, ambling, grazing caribou. Such is the wonder of the caribou migration.

Our use of the term "migration" often exposes our misunderstanding of the concept. We speak of the event as though it occurs during a limited period in the year of the caribou. In fact, these animals are nomadic. They rarely stay long in any location, following an ancient pattern, remaining steadily on the move to match their cycle of needs to the weather, flora, and geography of the land. Southern agriculturists could only dream of a nomadic grazing herd animal that managed its food resource in such a sustainable fashion.

for several winter homes used by a semi-permanent group of Copper Inuit. These people were driven south from the Arctic Ocean during the mini ice age that took place between the early 1500s and the 1800s. Needles and tools, more common to the Dene people who lived south of the tree line, were also found at the site, leading the archeologists to conclude that the Dene had a trading system in place. It is believed that the Inuit returned to Bathurst Inlet after the cold spell. Today, there are only about 30 people living in the community of Bathurst Inlet and another 60 at Bay Chimo, 63 miles, (100 km)to the north.

On one of his epic journeys, Sir John Franklin explored the area in 1821-22. After traversing the northern coast, he traveled along the river with a party of 20 men. It is difficult to imagine the travails of such

Caribou bull in fall colors.

RIGHT: *Caribou Antlers on Nadlock Island. These antlers were collected approximately 500 years ago and carried to the island. Anthropologists are unsure if they were incorporated in shelter construction or used as a defensive structure to keep out marauders.*

OPPOSITE PAGE: *Skin tents at Bathurst Inlet Lodge. The community surrounding the lodge has an economic incentive to preserve cultural knowledge.*

a journey with the primitive means of the day. On the overland portions of the route, the party carried small bark canoes. Tippy and fragile, they were relied on for crossing the rivers encountered along the way. The men had to carry them overhead while hiking, which proved trying as the boats caught the wind and drained the last energy from the marchers. Franklin and two of his crew tipped a little canoe while attempting to cross. One crewman named Belanger was marooned midriver while Franklin and the other member barely escaped. Belanger was finally rescued and treated for hypothermia. Fortunately the lives were saved but in the process, Franklin's journal was lost. Imagine keeping meticulous notes daily for more than a year, using a

〜〜〜〜〜〜〜〜〜〜〜〜〜〜〜〜〜〜
〜〜〜〜〜〜〜〜〜〜

NUNAVUT: A NEW TERRITORY

It is a curious situation that one-sixth of North America's landmass has undergone a major geopolitical division and that few people know anything about it.

The former expanse of the Northwest Territories represented more than one-third of Canada's landmass.

The aboriginal groups in the former NWT consist of the Dene, the Metis, and the Inuvialuit of the western Arctic and the Inuit of the Eastern Arctic. The cultural division between east and west is dramatic. Historically the two groups have maintained a healthy distance.

For many years the Inuit of the eastern Northwest Territories worked to create their own territory called Nunavut, which means "land of the people" in the Inuit language. This led to the establishment of two separate territorial governments within the former NWT. Ultimately the Inuit got their own territory. Nunavut territory and government was established on April 1, 1999, and has jurisdictional powers and fundamental institutions similar to the present Northwest Territories and Yukon Territory.

The Nunavut region is 136,291 square miles (352,994 sq. km). It was carved out of the NWT's former total of 742,889 square miles (1,924,082 sq. km). The selected land includes surface and subsurface rights with compensation for subsurface rights that were previously optioned by private industry.

The capital of Nunavut is Iqaluit on Baffin Island. Of the 60,000 residents formerly in the NWT, 17,500 currently reside within Nunavut.

bottle of ink and primitive pen. Then imagine trudging a distance greater than the width of the continent, carrying this journal in a wooden chest, only to have it disappear in a turbulent northern river. Such was the lot of John Franklin. Although he was able to capture details from records kept by his officers, it is likely that on that day, he may have regretted it was the journal that drowned and not him. The rapids were named after Belanger in commemoration of the disastrous crossing of the river.

It wasn't until 1920 that a permanent settlement was established at Bathurst Inlet. In that year, the explorer Charles Klengenburg wintered his crew and schooner at the inlet. Fourteen years later the Hudson's Bay Company established a trading post there. Later, the community grew around a mineral-exploration site

established in 1929. In 1964, the HBC pulled out of Bathurst Inlet. The post was then used as an RCMP post and later as an Anglican mission. It was subsequently purchased by retired RCMP officer Glen Warner and his wife, Trish, of Yellowknife, who turned it into a wildlife viewing facility called Bathurst Inlet Lodge. The Inuit families living in the community today have chosen an isolated and traditional way of life. However, in the summer the community, in conjunction with the Warners, operate Bathurst Inlet Lodge. The lodge is renowned worldwide as a naturalist's retreat.

Arctic cotton grass blooming and blowing in the breeze.

CHAPTER 9

Coppermine River (Nunavut, Northwest Territories): Bloody Fall

The Indians who are now appointed your guides, are to conduct you to the borders of the Athapuskow Indians country, where Captain Matonabbee is to meet you in the spring of one thousand seven hundred and seventy, in order to conduct you to a river represented by the Indians to abound with copper ore, animals of the fur kind, &c., and which is said to be so far to the Northward, that in the middle of the summer the sun does not set, and is supposed by the Indians to empty into some ocean. This river, which is called by the Northern Indians Neetha-sans-san-dazey, or the Far Of Metal River, you are if possible, to trace to the mouth, and there determine the latitude and longitude as near as you can; but more particularly so if you find it navigable, and that a settlement can be made there with any degree of safety, or benefit to the Company. "Be careful to observe what mines are near the river, what water there is at the river's mouth, how far the woods are from the seaside, the course of the river, the nature of the soil, and the production of it; and make other remarks that you may think will be either necessary or satisfactory. And if the said river be likely to be of any utility, take possession of it on behalf of the Hudson's Bay Company, by cutting your name on some of the rocks, as also the date of the year, month, &c.

Orders and Instructions for Mr. Samuel Hearne, going on an expedition by land towards the Latitude 70 North, in order to gain a knowledge of the Northern Indians Country, &c. on Behalf of the Honorable Hudson's Bay Company in the Year 1769.

The canyon and whitewater of Bloody Fall. It was here, at the apex of his journey, that Samuel Hearne witnessed a massacre in 1771. The natural hydraulics of the river provide a strategic location for catching arctic char.

The origin of the Coppermine lies far to the south at Lac de Gras, Northwest Territories. Here, in the scraped Precambrian Shield limestone basin, the water is uncommonly pure and clear. Roughly the first one-third

~~~~~~

~~~~~~~~~~~~~~~~

Origin: Lac de Gras, Northwest Territories

Length: 845 kilometers, 530 miles

Drop: 1,400 feet, (427 m)

Completion: Coronation Gulf of the Arctic Ocean at the community of Kugluktuk, Nunavut

Local inhabitants, Maegan and Tyson Klengenberg (opposite) of Kugluktuk greet river travelers. Beautiful soapstone carvings by Gordon Ihumatak (overleaf) depict the local culture, history, and lifestyle are one of the regions few exports.

of the river comprises chains of lakes. The midnight-sun conditions of the summer warm the water in the shield country. Willow and small shrubs dominate the vegetation with the occasional "krumholz" spruce, so designated because of the stunted condition due to strong winds.

Departing the lakes, the Coppermine rolls through low-lying hills. Cutting through one rise, a chasm named Rocky Defile provides wild water at some flow levels. Unique phenomena await along the way. At Stony Creek, springs that continue to run during the winter form sheets of auffice, a sort of mini glacier. In recent years the existence of the ice sheets in the summer has been sporadic, another possible sign of climate change.

Flanked with cliffs of sandstone and clay, the river is home to nesting raptors: peregrine and gyrfalcons, rough-legged hawks, as well as golden and bald eagles. Caribou, grizzly, muskoxen, wolverines, wolves, and foxes roam the tundra. World-class arctic char fishing, as well as trout and whitefish, await the traveler.

Dropping over a series of challenging rapids, the river flows north toward the Coronation Gulf of the Arctic Ocean. Just short of the estuary, the Coppermine squeezes through a beautiful canyon and falls. The area is known for quantities of native copper. A watchful traveler walking on shore may be lucky enough to spot a copper spear point. Law dictates that these artifacts must be left in place, although the traveler can note a

Global Positioning System (GPS) reading and report the find to the Prince of Wales Museum in Yellowknife.

For 3,500 years, the wider region has been home to the hunter/gatherer cultures of Copper Inuit in the north, and Athapaskan Slavey, Chipewyan, and Dogrib Indians to the south. These peoples followed a nomadic existence within this region, moving as dictated by the seasons to best harvest the bounty of the land. The Inuit dominated the northern region, to the edge of the Polar Sea. The Indians, now collectively named Dene, occupied the lands to the south.

Samuel Hearne first explored its lower reaches in 1771, prospecting for copper under the employ of the Hudson's Bay Company. He approached the river on foot in a journey of epic proportion. His trek began far to the east, on the shores of Hudson Bay; the Hudson's Bay Company occupied the trading establishment of the Prince of Wales Fort. It was here that a rumor was heard of a large quantity of copper on the banks of a great river. As history would have it, the task of exploration fell to a young navy veteran of the recent Seven Years War, who had worked at the fort for three years. Samuel Hearne was to locate the river and the copper prospect while mapping and "taking possession" of the river should it "be of any utility." Thus began an epic journey of modest means but heroic proportions.

After two problematic false starts in 1769 and 1770, Hearne embarked for the final time in the fall of 1770. Guided by a Chipewyan leader, Matonabbee,

Elder Mamie Oniak.

and an entourage that at times numbered upward of 200 men, women, and children, Hearne headed west. For seven months they crossed the tundra, living off the land. It was a Spartan existence. In his expedition journal, Hearne made the following observation of food: "Sometimes we had too much, seldom just enough, frequently too little and often none at all." After nearly ten months of travel, Hearne intersected the river at Sandstone Rapids not more than 38 miles (60 km) from its terminus, upstream of the place he later named Bloody Fall. As they progressed, Hearne observed that his guides were making preparation for battle. The Chipewyan believed that when one of their leaders died, the magic of the Eskimos was to blame. To avenge these deaths, they carried out bloody raids. Apparently there remained a debt unpaid at that time. En route, the Chipewyans had learned of a camp of Eskimos to the north, likely close to the river. Despite the protestations of Hearne, his group fell upon the Eskimo fishing encampment below a beautiful canyon

LEFT AND OPPOSITE PAGE: *The rich red flesh of the char is a key element of the Inuvialuit diet. The fish are gutted and "split," remaining attached at the tail. The meat is hung over a pole to dry, flesh side out. Kids playing around the drying fish will toss rocks at marauding ravens and other intruders who are attracted to the food. Among sport fishers, the Coppermine is known as a world-class char fishing destination. Samual Kikpak is shown drying Arctic Char.*

and falls. On July 17, 1771, the Eskimos were massacred. Hearne ignored the traditional place name of Kuklok and called the place Bloody Fall. Later he completed the final 15 kilometers (8 miles) to the Coronation Gulf of the Arctic Ocean. In spite of his doubts that the river or sea would be of any use, he erected a cairn to claim the coast on behalf of the Hudson's Bay Company.

After turning around, it took the group nearly one year to make their way back to the fort, arriving on June 30, 1772. Unfortunately Hearne's measurement of latitude was inaccurate and highly criticized at home in England.

Nearly fifty years later, Sir John Franklin, in the service of the Royal Navy, left Old Fort Providence, near present-day Yellowknife, guided by the Indian chief,

Akaitcho, and set out for the Arctic coastline. With his crew of French Canadians and English officers (Dr. John Richardson, Midshipmen George Black and Robert Hood) he explored the entire length of the Coppermine by canoe, arriving at the mouth of the river and Polar Sea in late July.

After exploring the Arctic coast as far east as Bathurst Inlet, Franklin returned overland to Fort Enterprise—a horrific journey marked by murder, starvation, and cannibalism, during which half his party died. Despite the tragic conclusion to his expedition, Franklin succeeded in exploring a large region of the Arctic and became the first white man to canoe the Coppermine River. He noted that the locations mapped by Hearne were just as he had recorded, redeeming his reputation posthumously, regardless of Hearne's poor estimations of latitude and longitude.

Although many parties have traveled the river in the 176 years since Sir John Franklin made his trip, little has changed in those intervening years. The adventurer of today experiences the land much as Hearne, Franklin, and the native people did almost two centuries ago.

Kugluktuk—New Name for the Hamlet of Coppermine

In the final phase of our Coppermine River expeditions we arrive at the Coronation Gulf of the Arctic Ocean. Here we are greeted by the friendly residents of Kugluktuk (formerly known as Coppermine). In the Nunavut Handbook Millie Kuliktana reports that the name was intended to mean "the place of moving water" in Inuinaktun.

"However, something was lost in the naming process and the proper spelling, Qurluqtuq, fell by the wayside. Klugluktuk actually means 'two startled people'! The community's peaceful demeanor, though, is unlikely to startle newcomers."

She goes on to state that the Inuit of this area are known as the Copper Inuit, a name born of the nearby Copper Mountains. Many hunters still use local copper to fashion tools, a valuable asset for a people that spend many months hunting and fishing. By spending so much time on the land, the Inuit of Kugluktuk ensure their traditional skills are passed on to younger generations, whether it be sewing fur clothing, hunting wild game, carving soapstone, preparing traditional food, drum dancing, or enjoying good old-time fiddling.

Full moon over Hamlet at 12:00 a.m.

CHAPTER 10

Horton River (Northwest Territories): The Smoking Hills

"My father used to tell me to respect the land and look after it. He said the land was like the white man's bank. When the white man needs something he goes to the bank; we get what we need from the land."
—JAMES POKIAK, INUVIALUIT RIVER GUIDE

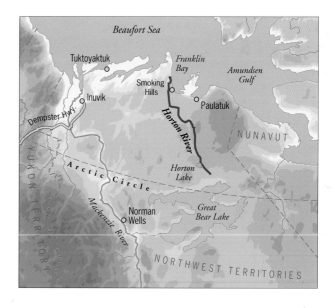

The Horton, mainland Canada's most northerly river, is a large but gentle waterway. Flowing through the tundra, it winds its way north to Amundson's Gulf on the Arctic Ocean. Even by the Northwest Territories' standards, the Horton River journey is as remote a river trip as one is likely to enjoy on mainland North America. Even the Inuit of Paulatuk, the nearest community, rarely travel this far. Those who travel the Horton will find its flora and fauna fascinating. The river's history, geography, and geology are also remarkable.

Sparse stands of black spruce are located along the riverbanks for the first 125 miles (200 km) downstream of Horton Lake, the river's headwaters. Willows continue through to the coast. The warmth of summer brings an explosion of color to the tundra. The trees virtually disappear as one heads farther north toward the ocean, with the exception of willows and other shrubs that seldom grow more than 3 feet (1 m) in height.

The fauna of the Horton include the 115,000 caribou of the Bluenose herd. Caribou are the only members of the deer family in which both the bulls and cows grow antlers. However, each sex grows them at different times. The cows have antlers while pregnant which allow them to poke bulls competing with them for food. The bulls' antlers reach their maximum length during the rutting season when the males must compete for mating privileges. After calving in the spring, at the apex of their migration, the cows and calves make their way northwest to rendezvous

Canoeists enjoy the frequent wildlife sightings. Here a caribou of the Bluenose herd watches as they paddle by.

Origin: Horton Lake, Northwest
Territories

Length: 373 miles (600 km)

Drop: 1135 feet (346 m)

Completion: Franklin Bay on
the Arctic Ocean

Unique Status:

The river was shortened by 15
miles (25 km) about 150 years
ago when a new channel eroded
the east bank of the river near
its mouth

with the bulls that do not migrate as far. Foraging as
they go, they feed and fatten along the way. Among the
many perils that await them en route are river crossings,
hungry wolves, predatory golden eagles, grizzlies, and
tortuous botflies, which hatch larvae in the caribou's nostrils, and warble fly larvae that grow under the skin. Still,
the caribou have adapted masterfully to the environment; their instinctive strategies match their migratory
lifestyle. As previously mentioned, the caribou maintain
safety by moving as a herd. Adhering to the adage of
safety in numbers, they group together. So strong is the
grouping instinct that a river traveler can attract a lone
caribou by slowly waving her extended arms overhead in
the air, mimicking the appearance of antlers.

Wolves, foxes, and grizzly bears tail the caribou herd.
The wolves den throughout the range and intercept the
migration. Caribou meat sustains them in birthing and
raising their pups. Foxes clean up the remains of wolf
kills and hunt for smaller mammals such as lemmings,
ground squirrels (known locally as sics) and mice.
Grizzly bears intercept the herd as it passes through their
territory. They seek out sick or injured animals and
chase them down.

Peregrine falcons, golden eagles, rough-legged
hawks, and a host of other bird species delight the
birder. The populations of raptors can fluctuate with
that of the small rodents on which they feed. Of course
one airborne species is ever present: the dreaded mos-
quito. But there are times of reprieve. This is a land

The Smoking Hills near
Franklin Bay.

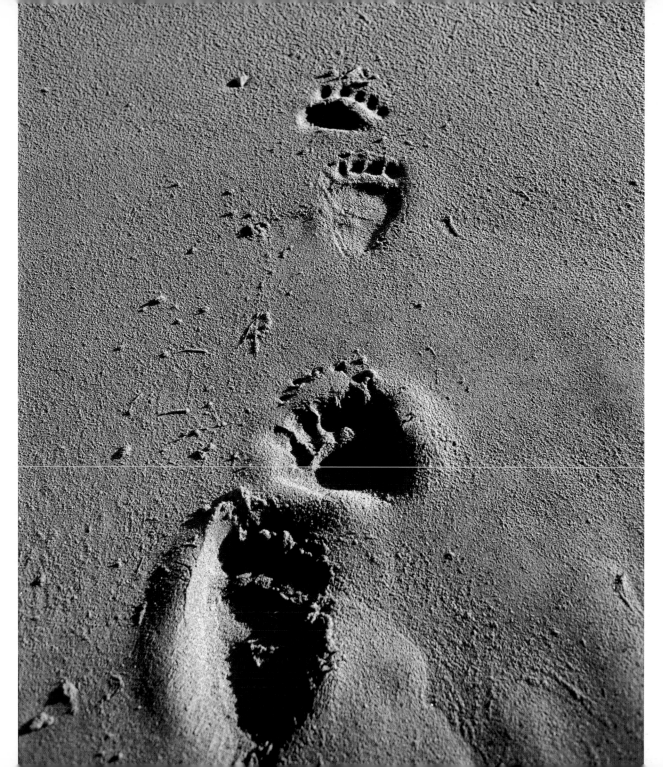

LEFT: *Crystal Caves along the Horton.*

RIGHT: *Grizzly tracks.*

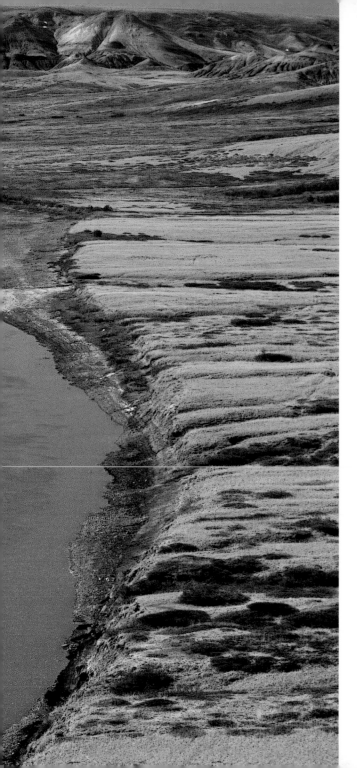

where the weather often changes dramatically within a given day. When the winds blow, the mosquitoes disappear. When the air calms and warms, the hordes emerge and river travelers don the ubiquitous tundra uniform—a bug shirt.

The Horton itself starts off as a clear, swift-flowing river; but it grows more voluminous and murky as one heads toward the coastline. This is particularly true in the early season when the floodwaters are still up. There are a few whitewater challenges on the Horton, almost all of which occur in a brief 25-mile (40-km) canyon section, near the halfway point.

Fishing is generally good along most of the river during the latter part of July, once the floodwaters dissipate. Lake trout and grayling are the species commonly caught. There is an arctic char run later in the summer months.

Below the canyon, at Coal Creek, one can find the remains of a cabin built by Vilhjalmur Stefansson, a circumpolar explorer, geographer and anthropologist. In one of his most famous books *My Life with the Eskimo* (1913), he provided a detailed account of the skills and knowledge he acquired while living with the Inuvialuit people in the Arctic. In the sparse tundra setting, the cabin remains are an inspiring testimony to the adaptability of this explorer who had the wisdom to learn subsistence skills from the local people.

Archeologists report that the Horton was once inhabited by Thule people, who migrated to the region

Canoeing the gentle flowing Horton River, Northwest Territory.

Deadfall trap used in the past for trapping wolverine and fox.

from Alaska between 1100 and 1400 AD. The Inuvialuit, who inhabit the nearest community of Paulatuk (located approximately 62 miles (100 km) east of the river), migrated to the area with Euro-American whalers in the 19th century. The Hareskin Dene also lived in the region, likely to the south in an uneasy coexistence with the coastal peoples. The Hareskin are now chiefly centered in Coleville Lake, a small community about 100 miles (160km) west of Horton Lake.

Hiking opportunities abound in the tundra environment, along the entire length of the river. For much of the route the Horton has carved a distinct valley through sedimentary substrate, unlike the other tundra rivers mentioned in this book that flow over unyielding Precambrian rock. If you hike to the crest of the valley, you can see sweeping vistas over the rolling landscape. The opportunity to look as far as the eye can see in any direction, with no sign of human enterprise, is a wilderness luxury.

As it nears the coast and runs parallel to it, the river begins to loop in large meanders, which seem to reach for the sea and then curve back inland. Between the river and the ocean is a range of low-lying hills. It is possible to take a day's hike through the hills to the coast and discover an otherworldly phenomenon. At the top of cliffs overlooking the ocean, billowing plumes of sulfurous-smelling smoke roll across the landscape. The fumaroles are the result of concentrations of microscopic pyrites, rich in sulfur within the

carbon-rich shale near the surface. This combination ignites spontaneously with oxygen. The acrid, foul-smelling smoke billows and rolls across the coastal tundra for nearly 25 miles (40 km) yielding an acid rain-like landscape. Only specialized plants can survive within the shadow of the acidic smoke. This region is known as the Smoking Hills and links the modern traveler with a historic exploration. The river is named after Wilmet Horton, the undersecretary of state for the British Colonial Department, by Dr. John Richardson of the Franklin Expedition. Richardson was the expedition team's surgeon-naturalist. He accompanied Franklin and his men during their search for the Northwest Passage. They explored the shores of Franklin Bay in 1826 and noted the billowing plumes of sulfurous-smelling smoke from the ridge tops. At first the smoke must have appeared as a confusing specter, leading them to believe they were seeing campfires lining the coastal hills. The phenomenon has persisted for hundreds of years, and predates Richardson's visit. Modern travelers are able to marvel at the Smoking Hills while they search for seals and beluga whales off the coast with the help of binoculars.

The terminus of the river in the Arctic Ocean has undergone a relatively recent evolution. Approximately 150 years ago, the last large meander breached the neck of land, which separated it from the ocean. This became the final egress of the river, and the meander was abandoned along with the extensive delta land that

had grown over the millennia. Compared with neigh-
boring northern rivers, the Horton has a distinctly clear
entry to the ocean. This will change, of course, over
time. But for now it provides a small window of observation into the ongoing life and evolution of a wild and
free river.

Old Sulpher Vents at 2:00 a.m.

Glossary of Northern Terms

The North is full of distinctive and even exotic natural phenomena. And we have a delightful array of terms to describe them. Being familiar with these terms adds another dimension to one's experience of the North. Besides, some of the words are absolutely sensuous. Try rolling "alluvial" off the tip of your tongue.

The best introduction to these phenomena is E. C. Pielou's *A Naturalist's Guide to the Arctic*. We carry a copy on every trip. I have also compiled a glossary of geological phenomena one encounters in the North, which appears below.

(Definitions taken from American Geological Institute [1962], Fairbridge 1968, Brown and Kupsch [1974], Washburn [1973], and Canada Soil Survey Committee [1996]) "Ecoregions of Yukon Territory" by E.T. Oswald and J.P. Senyk and was published by Environment Canada and the Canadian Forestry Service in 1977.)

American Geological Institute. 1962. Dictionary of Geological Terms. Doubleday and Company Inc. Garden City, New York.

Brown, R.J.E. and W.O. Kupsch. 1974. Permaforst Terminology. Tech. Mem. No. 111, NRCC 14274

Washburn, A.L. 1973. Periglacial Processes and Environments. St. Martin's Press. New York.

Canada Soil Suvey Committee. 1976. The Canadian System of Soil Classification. Agriculture Canada. Publ. 1455 Draft Revision.

Active layer: In permafrost regions, the layer of ground above the permafrost table that thaws each summer and refreezes each fall.

Aeolian: Materials transported and deposited by wind action. Generally consist of medium-to-fine sand and coarse silt.

Alluvium: Material of any particle size that has been deposited by moving water.

Aufeis: A sheet-like mass of ice on the ground or on the surface of river ice. It is generated by repeated flooding and refreezing of a river during the winter,

Single Otter on McClusky Lake, the launching point for the Wind River, follows a scenic mountain flight.

creating a build-up of new ice layers. (we sometimes spot this during the summer on the banks of side streams).

Beaded stream: A drainage pattern of individual streams in which pools or small lakes are connected by short stream reaches. The melting of ground ice causes the pools.

Bog: Peat-covered areas or peat-filled depressions with a high water table, strongly acid peat, and surface layer of mosses.

Brunisol: A type of soil with weak development; it is often light brown in color with good drainage and of a loam or coarser texture.

Cat steps (Terracettes): Narrow ledges of earth on steep hillsides. In instances cited, likely due to landslip aided by freeze-thaw action.

Circle: A circular-patterned ground formation that is the result of long-term movement of rock, powered by the freeze-thaw mechanics and differential heating and thawing.

Non-sorted Circle: Patterned ground feature occurring in groups, whose interior surface is dominantly circular and lacks a border of stone.

Sorted Circle: Patterned ground feature, occurring in groups, whose interior surface is dominantly circular and which has a sorted appearance commonly due to a border of stones surrounding finer material.

Cirque: A bowl-shaped, hollow recess in a mountain resulting from glacial ice erosion.

Coluvium: Materials of any particle size that have reached their present position by direct gravity-induced movement.

Cryoturbation: A collective term to describe all soil movements due to frost action. Encompasses frost heaving and all differential and mass movement including expansion and contraction due to temperature change.

Deglaciation: Uncovering of the land surface brought about by the melting of glacier ice. It would seem that the entire planet is currently in this phase.

Drumlin: A smooth, streamlined cigar-shaped hill formed beneath moving glacial ice.

Drunken forest: A group of trees leaning in a random orientation usually associated with thermokarst topography.

Eco-region: An area of land where the vegetation, soils, and permafrost reflect the regional climate.

Ericaceous plants: A collective term for members of the *Ericacea* family; shrubby plants with usually thick leathery leaves.

Felsenmeer: A chaotic assemblage of fractured, often upheaved, rocks resulting from intensive frost shattering of jointed bedrock.

Fen: A peatland with slowly moving water above or below the surface,

Forbs: A general term used to refer to non-woody plants other than graminoids, mosses and lichens.

Frost cracking: Fracturing of the ground by thermal contraction at temperatures below 0°C.

Frost table: Any frozen surface within the active layer above the permafrost table or a frozen surface in seasonally frozen ground in a non-permafrost environment.

Glacio-fluvial: Materials deposited by moving water either in front of, or in contact with, glacier ice.

Glacio-lacustrine: Materials originating from glacier ice and deposited in standing water.

Graminoid vegetation: A collective term for grasses, sedges, cotton grass, bulrushes, reeds, etc.

Hummock: special non-sorted form of net, characterized by a knob-like shape and vegetation cover.
    Earth hummock—hummocks having a core of mineral soil. Turf hummock—hummocks consisting of vegetation with or without a core of mineral soil or stone.

Ice contact: Material dropped in holes, ice-walled trenches, etc., and remains on the land surface when the glacier melts.

Ground ice: Ice in pores, cavities, voids, or other openings in soil or rock, including massive ice.

Segregated ice: Ice formed by the migration of pore water to the freezing plane where it forms into discrete lenses, layers, or seams ranging in thickness from hairline to greater than 33ft (10 m).

Ice lens: A dominantly horizontal lens-shaped body of ice of any dimension. Commonly used for layers of segregated ice that are parallel to the ground surface.

The lenses may range in thickness from a hairline to as much as about 33ft (10 m).

Ice wedge: In permafrost regions, a massive, generally wedge-shaped body with its apex pointing downward, composed of layered, vertically oriented, commonly white ice; from less than 4 in (10 cm) to 10 ft (3 m) or more wide at the top, tapering to a feather edge at the apex at a depth of 3 to 33 ft (1 to 10 m) or more. Some ice wedges may extend downward as far as 82 ft (25 m).

Kame: Mounds of poorly sorted, water-laden sand and gravel formed within holes or fissures in the glacier or between the glacier and the land surface.

Lapilli: Coarse ash, volcanic ejecta ranging in size from 0.156 to 1.3 in (4 mm to 32 mm).

Loess: Glacial till, highly ground to a fine dust, deposited by wind in thick beds.

Marl: Finely-textured (silts and clays) highly calcareous unconsolidated material containing shells.

Moraine: Rock debris ranging from clay to large block size, which has been transported beneath, beside, or within and in front of moving ice and deposited on the land surface during both growth and recession of the ice and not modified by any intermediate agent.

Lateral moraine: elongated accumulation of rock and soil debris lying on the surface of a glacier in a valley at or near the lateral margin of the glacier.

Medial moraine: elongated accumulation of rock and soil debris formed by the joining of adjacent lateral moraines below the juncture of the two valley glaciers.

Nivation hollows: Bowl-shaped depressions caused by frost action and mass wasting beneath lingering or perennial snowdrifts.

Oriented lake: One of a number of lakes having a parallel alignment and commonly elliptical or rectangular in plan. [We often observe these lakes on the tundra caused by glacial scouring, from the air as we fly in to begin our river trip.]

Palsa: A round or elongated hillock or mound, maximum height of about 10 m, composed of a peat layer overlying mineral soil. It has a perennially frozen core which extends from within the covering peat layer downward into or toward the underlying mineral soil.

Peat: Colloquial term: Muskeg—Unconsolidated, compressible material consisting of partially decomposed, semi-carbonized remains of plants such as mosses, sedges and trees, some animal residues, and commonly some mineral soil.

Peat mound: A mound or hillock in a peatland composed mainly of peat overlying mineral soil.

Peat plateau: A low, generally flat-topped expanse of peat, rising 3 or more ft (1 or more m) above the general surface of a peatland. A layer of permafrost exists in the peat plateau, which may extend into the peat below the general peatland surface and even into the underlying mineral soil.

Peatland: Any terrain covered by a layer of peat.

Permafrost: The thermal condition of soil or rock of having temperatures below 32°F (0°C) persist over at least two consecutive winters and the intervening summer. Permafrost occurring everywhere beneath the exposed land surface throughout a geographic regional zone with the exception of widely scattered sites.

Permafrost, discontinuous: permafrost occurring in some areas beneath the ground surface throughout a geographic regional zone where other areas are free of permafrost.

Permafrost, widespread: Permafrost that is widely distributed but not continuous beneath the land surface.

Permafrost table: The upper boundary of permafrost.

Permafrost thickness: The vertical distance between the permafrost table and the permafrost base.

Pingo: A conical, commonly more or less asymmetrical mound or hill, with a circular or oval base and commonly fissured summit, which has a core of massive ground ice covered with soil and vegetation, and which exists for at least two winters.

Pingo, closed system: A generic term for a pingo, in flat, poorly drained terrain of the continuous permafrost zone, which originates where a water-bearing, unfrozen layer of soil, generally in a thaw basin underlying a lake, becomes enclosed by permafrost aggradations (as when a previously existing lake, which provided insulation, shallows or drains completely) causing the expulsion of pore water. The water may dome up the overlying permafrost and inject water that freezes into that layer to form the ice-cored pingo, or the overlying permafrost may be domed up by the segregation of ice.

Pingo, open system: A generic term for a pingo in areas of marked relief mainly in the discontinuous permafrost zone. An open system pingo originates where the hydrostatic pressure of water circulating from higher ground to beneath a frozen layer causes injection of water, which freezes into a weakened part of the overlying layer to form the ice-cored pingo.

Polygon: A type of patterned ground consisting of a closed, roughly equidimensional figure bounded by several sides, commonly more or less straight but some, or all, of which may be irregularly curved.

Polygon, high center: A polygon having a center that is higher than its margins.

Polygon, low center: A polygon having a center that is lower than its margins.

Polygon, non-sorted: Patterned ground whose mesh is dominantly polygonal and lacks a border of stones.

Pro-glacial: Material carried beyond the glacial margins.

Rock glacier: A glacier-like tongue of angular rock waste usually heading in cirques or other steep-walled hollows.

Scree: A sheet of coarse debris mantling a mountain slope. A frost-riven rubble sheet consisting of angular rocks with few lines, resulting from freeze-thaw action and downslope creep.

Seral: Any stage in the succession of plants from pioneers following disturbances to the climax vegetation.

Solifluction: The process of slow, gravitational downslope movement of saturated, unfrozen earth material behaving apparently as a viscous mass over a surface of frozen material. *Solifluction features*: Physiographic features of varying scale produced by the process of solifluction, which include lobe, stripe, sheet, terrace.

Step: Patterned ground features occurring in groups displaying a step-like form and downslope border of vegetation or stones embanking an area of relatively bare ground up-slope.

Stone net: A type of patterned ground characterized by a textural differentiation caused by the frost action between fine-grained soils in the center and coarse-grained, stony materials forming the rims of an irregular network of features intermediate between sorted circles and sorted polygons.

String bog (fen): Boggy area marked by serpentine ridges of peat and vegetation, interspersed with depressions, many of which contain shallow ponds.

Stripe, non-sorted: Patterned ground with a striped pattern and a non-sorted appearance owing to parallel lines of vegetation-covered ground and intervening strips of relatively bare ground oriented down the steepest available slope.

Thermokarst (topography): The irregular topography resulting from the process of differential thaw settlement or caving of the ground because of the melting of ground ice.

Tor: Isolated masses of rock protruding above the surrounding landscape and consisting of either a single or numerous joint blocks displaying varying degrees of angularity and roundness. Probably more resistant to weathering than the surrounding terrain.

Tundra: A treeless, generally level to undulating, region of lichens, mosses, sedges, grasses, and some low shrubs, including dwarf willows and birches, which is characteristic of both the Arctic and higher alpine regions outside of the Arctic.

The Spell of the Yukon

There's a land where the mountains are nameless,-
And the rivers all run God knows where;
There are lives that are erring and aimless,
And deaths that just hang by a hair;
There are hardships that nobody reckons;
There are valleys unpeopled and still;
There's a land oh it beckons and beckons,
And I want to go back—and I will.
—Robert W. Service

OPPOSITE PAGE: *The ramparts of the Nahanni Plateau. The flight upriver before the river trip begins is spectacular. Upon disembarking from the Twin Otter visitors often say, "If my trip ended now, I'd already have had my money's worth!"*

LEFT: *Muskox can be viewed on the Burnside, Coppermine, Horton and Firth rivers. The large horn covering the skull is known as a "boss."*

ABOVE: *The seldom seen and rarely photographed wolverine is a good sign of a healthy ecosystem.*

Conclusion: Confluence

The great rivers of the North are among the most magnificent sights on this planet. Terry Parker's images reveal how these beautiful waterways cut through the heart of the features that collectively form the magnetic North. Happily they have been spared some of the abuse to which most waterways are subjected. Paddling or floating along these world-class rivers, is truly a marvelous experience. It is difficult to imagine undertaking such a trip without having a great respect for the sacredness of these rivers. I sometimes muse on the wisdom of sharing them with our southern visitors. Why reveal these treasures? Would they not be better preserved if left unvisited? The truth is no. In fact, it has been the visitors, and in many cases, only the visitors, who have defended the integrity of these waterways and wild lands against errant plans for "development." People will protect what they love. It may take books like this to awaken readers to the uniqueness and fragility of this land, but you can bet that such a lure is not necessary for resource extraction industries. Most people would agree that "if it can't be grown, it has to be mined," but this does not mean at all costs. Recent reports have itemized the large number of abandoned mining properties across the North requiring extensive reclamation work. Through the water table, these sites threaten the integrity of the rivers and living things. The regeneration of these sites alone would represent a major economic engine in the North. As for future extraction. It must be conducted with a watchful eye to its effects. It is a bad time to sell our resources when world markets are set by commodity prices based on extraction with third-world environmental strategies and practices. Have the developers not heard the adage "By low, sell high"? Let's not let our assets go in flea market conditions.

Although we can enjoy the pristine state of our northern rivers for now, we must be ever vigilant. With an ever-expanding network of roads and business communities that hunger for development projects, we are learning in this new millennium that the unspoiled state of these lands cannot be taken for granted. Environmental degradation that was once unthinkable due to the remoteness of the North is now possible. Moreover, civilization is beginning to encroach on wilderness areas in the form of more roads. We tell ourselves the few roads that do exist in the North have always been there, so what's one more? Yukon is an excellent example of this. Before the Second World War,

Alpine beauty of the Snake River.

~~~~~~
~~~~~~

it contained less than a few hundred miles of roads. With the sudden building of the Alcan highway, under the threat of wartime invasion, the momentum of development increased exponentially. Now a map of southern Yukon looks like the a spiderweb of cracks

> ### HOW TO GET THERE
> *Details for journeys on the 10 rivers described in this book can be found at www.nahanni.com or by contacting Nahanni River Adventures at info@nahanni.com Phone: 1 (800) 297-6927 or (867) 668-3180 Mailing address: P.O. Box 31203 Whitehorse, Yukon Territory, Canada Y1A 5P7*

across a Yukon windshield. With roads, the bitter reality is there is no going back. History has clearly demonstrated that once roads are built to provide access to remote areas, they begin to proliferate. Commercial development follows.

Other recent examples include the resurrection of an abandoned mine on the edge of Nahanni National Park. The new owners announced that the mine could only be made viable with the development of an all-weather road that would parallel the park boundary to a tributary flowing into the heart of the park. The impact on the South Nahanni ecosystem would be significant and perpetual. At the time of writing, this threat is unresolved.

Vigilance combined with sustainable resource planning and management will hopefully lead to greater assurance of a healthy future for our northern rivers. Politicians will generally follow the will of the voters. Sustainable tourism plays a vital role in informing the voters so that they understand what is at stake. Visionary land use planning is a concept few will protest. The challenge is to continually convince each succeeding government of the importance of this goal and the value of wild places. Economic models must be developed to show that wild rivers are worth more "alive" than "dead." Finally, those of us who have fallen in love with wild rivers must also lobby to protect them.

Acknowledgments

These stories would not have made it to print without the patient support of my wife and son, Judy and Lars. My parents, Roy and Lois, must also be commended for sacrificing their backyard to years of canoe building, among many other things.

It has been the nature of my work over the past two decades to distill the details of the rivers I guide people through and pass this information on to my guests as interpretive information. This book is based on knowledge I've accumulated over the course of twenty years, and for this reason the sources of some information have become cloudy or lost. Where possible I have followed the convention of acknowledging one's sources. I would also like to mention here that over the years I have received helpful input from:

Morten Asfeldt; Barry Beals; Chuck Blyth; Sophie Borcoman; Deborah Burgess of Good Earth Productions; Page Burt; Ric Careless; Steve Catto; Karmen Cheetham; Randy Clement; Ric Driediger; J. Raymond Edinger, Jr; Kathy Eliot; Tom Elliot; Gary Fiegehen; Dr. Derek Ford; Sarah Gaunt; Dr. Gary Gibson; Ted Grant; Deborah Griffith; Marilyn Hagerman; Bob Hanley; Lars Hartling; Stuart Herd; Mark Hume; Lawrence Joe; Peter Jowett; Bruce Kirkby; Mors Kochanski; Mark Lund; Russ Lyman; Hector Mackenzie; Henry and Lana Madsen; Ken Madsen; Ihor Macijiwsky of Good Earth Productions; Bill, Joyce, Paul, and Becky Mason; Richard E. Morlan, Canadian Museum of Civilization; Nahanni River Adventures Guides; Lynn E. Noel; Dick North; Joe Ordonez; Juri Peepri; James and Jacob Pokiak; Dona Reel; Dick Rice; Wally Schaber; Dr. Harvey Scott; Dr. George W. Scotter; Mike Speaks; Darielle Talarico; Jennifer Voss; Boyd Warner.

—NEIL HARTLING

Over the past 12 years I have continually strived to produce intriguing, striking and informative photography. To be able to capture such images you must be able to see the beauty, lighting, or composition of your subjects. But it is the reason you have chosen to be in that particular spot, about to record that moment when you truly define yourself as a photographer, and perhaps who you are as a person.

Who I am as a person certainly comes from my childhood growing up so close to my grandfather's farm, exploring its ponds and woodlots. My grandfather

OPPOSITE PAGE: *Aurora Borealis lights up the evening skies.*

ABOVE: *Sunset on the Back Bone Range. Snake River, Yukon.*

Ralph and father Tom taught me the ways of the woods (Southern Ontario woods anyway) as well as how to respect and conserve nature, and to them I am grateful. I would also like to thank the rest of the Parker family who have always believed in my work. Thanks of course to my always supportive mother Ruth, sisters Kim, Kristen and brother Mike. Also to Pat, Bill, Lois, Ginny and Sandy for being on this often challenging journey. To my deceased grandparents Beatrice Parker, Cecil and Breatice Wailes, I know you can see the beauty in these rivers as well.

There of course have been many people who have at one time or another helped me get to a location, posed for one or more pictures or simply helped me get my shot. Some have played major roles in getting my career established, and to them I thank: Air Tindi, Arctic Chalet B&B, Barry Beals, Brian Bell, Tim Boys, Colleen Bruce, Lona Collins, Custom Colour, First Air, Deni Gaccione, G.King Photo, GNWT, Andrea Graham, Ted Grant, Guides of Nahanni River Adventures, Bob Gurr, Monte Hummel, Inkit, Gary Jaeb, Cooper Langford, Marion Levigne, Jerry Loomis, NWTAT, Joey Olivieri, Outcrop, Parallel, Parks Canada, Patagonia, John Pekelsky, Richard Popko, Andy Russell, South Nahanni Air, Kaj Svensson, Roy Tanami, Up Here, Alasdair Veitch, Boyd Warner, Yukon Tourism, Dennis Zimmermann.

—TERRY PARKER

Gyrfalcon chicks in nest.